O9-AIG-086

WONDERWALKS

The Trails of New Jersey Audubon

Patricia Robinson

Margaret E. Heggan Free Public Library
208 East Holly Avenue
Hurffville, New Jersey 08080

Plexus Publishing, Inc.
Medford, New Jersey

First printing, 2003

Copyright © 2003 by Patricia Robinson

Published by: Plexus Publishing, Inc.
                  143 Old Marlton Pike
                  Medford, NJ 08055

All rights reserved. No part of this book may be reproduced in any
form without the written permission of the publisher.

Publisher's Note: The author and publisher have taken care in preparation
of this book but make no expressed or implied warranty of any kind and
assume no responsibility for errors or omissions. No liability is assumed for
incidental or consequential damages in connection with or arising out of
the use of the information contained herein.

Printed in the United States of America.

Library of Congress Cataloging-in-Publication Data

Robinson, Patricia (Patricia Claire)
   Wonderwalks : the trails of New Jersey Audubon / Patricia Robinson.
      p. cm.
Includes bibliographical references and index.
   ISBN 0-937548-53-7 (pbk.)
   1. Hiking--New Jersey--Guidebooks. 2. Nature study--New Jersey--
Guidebooks. 3. Wildlife refuges--New Jersey--Guidebooks. 4. Trails--
New Jersey--Guidebooks. 5. New Jersey--Guidebooks. 6. New Jersey
Audubon Society. I. Title: Wonder walks. II. Title.

   GV199.42.N5R64 2003
      917.4904'44--dc21
                                                      2003012957

Publisher: Thomas H. Hogan, Sr.
Editor-in-Chief: John B. Bryans
Managing Editor: Deborah R. Poulson
Sales Manager: Pat Palatucci
Graphics Department Director: M. Heide Dengler
Copy Editor: Pat Hadley-Miller
Book Designer: Kara Mia Jalkowski
Cover Designer: Erica Pannella
Indexer: Enid Zafran

Dedication

To Rich and Pat Kane, two very rare birds.
Thanks for coming to New Jersey!

Contents

Preface

There is a chain of green jewels gracing the New Jersey landscape from the Highlands to the Pinelands to the coast. These are the more than 30 New Jersey Audubon wildlife sanctuaries permanently protected for the enjoyment of the public and the conservation of wildlife habitat. From Sparta Mountain in Sussex County to Bennett Bog in Cape May, the sanctuaries feature verdant woods and wetlands, inviting trails, an abundance of birds and other wildlife, and endangered and rare plants and animals as well.

Pat Robinson's *Wonderwalks* is a delightful guide to most of New Jersey Audubon's green jewels. Take it with you in your travels around the state and experience the rich and rewarding treats awaiting you. There is a New Jersey Audubon sanctuary within 20 miles of nearly every citizen of the state. And there are nine New Jersey Audubon centers among them with helpful staff to enrich your explorations. Staff and volunteers can answer your questions, and in your travels you might well run into Pat Robinson!

Rich Kane,
Former Vice President, Conservation and Stewardship,
New Jersey Audubon Society

Margaret E. Heggan Free Public Library
208 East Holly Avenue
Hurffville, New Jersey 08080

Introduction:
Why Wonderwalks?

The winter of 2002 was a particularly warm one. On one, very springlike day in February, just for the fun of it, I took myself for a drive to New Jersey Audubon's Rancocas Nature Center, located in Burlington County, about an hour and a half from where I live.

It was early, so I had the trail all to myself, for a while. Eventually I met a man and woman who asked me if I knew where Rancocas State Park was. They were looking for the park when they came across the center and decided to stop. They told me they weren't birders; they "just wanted to take a walk" around the trail. Was that okay?

That's why I wrote *Wonderwalks*.

One of the oldest nonprofit conservation groups in the United States, the New Jersey Audubon Society has long been the protector of wildlife preserves with a collection of nature trails and environmental offerings, free to the public. All the same, it's been considered something of a birder's club.

Some of us are old enough to remember the "You don't have to be Jewish to like Levy's Rye Bread" commercials. Well, you don't have to be a birder to enjoy New Jersey Audubon's nature centers and sanctuaries. Never mind that the society has become the caretaker of more than 30 nature preserves and sanctuaries, including nine staffed nature centers, up and down the Garden State. Many of these properties offer free access to anyone who wants to enjoy them, whether they're birding, strolling, hiking, or just plain want to be alone with their thoughts.

There's just been one hitch: No commercial book ever collectively presented the sanctuaries and preserves under one cover. Not, that is, until now.

Hence, *Wonderwalks: The Trails of New Jersey Audubon*. The title was easy enough to choose. Scherman-Hoffman Wildlife Sanctuary, which I call my "home" sanctuary, has been offering "Wonderwalks" as part of their nature program for years. The two-hour walks, led by a naturalist, encourage participants to open their eyes and discover the flora and fauna around them.

One word on how to use this book: *Wonderwalks* is separated into two parts. Part One lists all the staffed nature centers from the Highlands in the North down to Cape May in the South. Part Two lists preserves that are readily accessible to the public. (Note: Not all preserves have workable trails, so I have included those that are easily accessible.) Pertinent information in each chapter includes the hours centers and preserves are open, facilities they provide (if any), and directions on how to get there. Also, centers are individualistic and vary in the depth of their trail information. Some, like Scherman-Hoffman, are extensive. Others, like the new Plainsboro Preserve, are still in the fact-finding stage.

Each nature center in Part One also contains lists pertaining to its local "specialty." Most entries have bird lists, broken out by season for easier identification. Others have wildflower lists and lists for mammals and reptiles, butterflies, trees and shrubs. Again, center lists are not consistent.

One word about bird lists: I have tried to keep the lists as simple as possible, breaking them down in alphabetical order and according to the season in which you are apt to see the birds. I did this to provide some consistency to the lists and to make them as first-time user friendly as possible.

With this book, you can enjoy your own wonderwalks. Use it in good health!

Patricia Robinson

Acknowledgments

This book could not have been produced without the help of my numerous friends at New Jersey Audubon who, many times, were deluged with questions, phone calls, e-mails, and spot visits to be sure I had everything I needed to make the book as enjoyable as possible.

That said, a big thank you to Tom Gilmore, president of New Jersey Audubon Society, for giving me the blessing and backing to write it; Rich Kane, as always, for his guidance and for writing the preface; Mike Anderson for eyeballing the bird lists.

Also, thanks to Philip De Rea, Jeff Birdsill, Karl Anderson, Pete Bacinski, Don Freiday, Brian Vernachio, Eric Stiles, Gretchen Ferrante, Sue Ann Slotterback, Pete Dunne, Sheila Lego, and Kathy Iozzo for humoring my "stealth" attacks at the centers; and Frank Lenik for the great tour of Twin Islands and the Rancocas side trips.

Finally, to the good people at Plexus, especially Editor-in-Chief John Bryans, who believed in the idea; and to Managing Editor Deborah Poulson, who had the thankless task of performing her editing magic on the final work.

Part I

The Staffed
Nature Centers

*New Jersey Audubon has nine staffed nature centers.
From the mountains and forests of the Highlands
in the north to the flat wetlands of the southern
Coastal Plains, visitors can enjoy every kind of
environment the Garden State has to offer.*

*Most of the centers are located on property deeded to
New Jersey Audubon by private, environmentally conscious
citizens over the years. Others, like the Plainsboro Preserve
and Sandy Hook Bird Observatory, are the results of
collaborations with either local (Plainsboro) or federal
(Sandy Hook) authorities. In all cases, trails and facilities
are maintained by professional naturalists and volunteers
who have extensive knowledge of their surroundings.*

Chapter One

Weis Ecology Center:
Roughing It in the Highlands

HISTORY

Weis Ecology came under the ownership of New Jersey Audubon in 1995, following a 21-year sojourn as a private environmental center, owned and managed by Walter and May Weis. Today the focus is on educating the public on environmental and ecological awareness.

It is also the only New Jersey Audubon site that offers camping facilities on the premises. The rustic, one- and two-room cabins have no modern sanitary facilities, but do provide an adventure, especially when bears wander through the grounds!

TERRAIN

The center sits buried in a pine and hardwood forest in the New Jersey Highlands adjacent to Norvin Green

3

Weis Ecology Center
150 Snake Den Road
Ringwood, NJ 07456
Phone: (973) 835-2160
E-mail: weis@
njaudubon.org

Hours: Wednesday
through Sunday, 8:30
A.M. to 4:30 P.M.
Closed Mondays,
Tuesdays, and major
holidays. Trails open
daily 9 A.M. to dusk.

Facilities: Visitor
Center with book and
gift store, special
events room for
art/photography
exhibits, butterfly
garden and meadows,
aviary that houses
injured birds of prey,
campsites, and one-
and two-room cabins.

Visitor's Center

State Forest. As luck would have it, the center's trails feed into the park's 24-mile hiking network. This is the tip of the Highlands, which means the bulk of the trails are rugged and steep. Anyone adventurous enough to come here will find either an easy ramble or a vigorous hike.

TRAILS

Weis's focus is not so much on birds, but on presenting nature, the environment, and conservation in an enjoyable manner. The center's programs range from hikes to children's activities to adult classes on cross-country skiing.

But the natural emphasis is on hiking. To help visitors, Weis suggests five routes that range from a comfortable walk to super-strenuous.

How to Get Here

From the South via Route 287: Take Route 287 North to Exit 55. Turn right onto Ringwood Avenue and proceed four miles until you reach Westbrook Road. Bear to the left at the fork and take the second left onto Snake Den Road. Follow signs to the center and park in the lower parking lot.

From the South via the Garden State Parkway: Follow the parkway north to Exit 155P (Route 19 North). Follow Route 19 to Route 80 West to Route 23 North. From Route 23 North proceed to Route 287 North and follow the above directions.

From the West via Route 80: Take Route 80 East to Route 287 North and follow the above directions.

From the East via the George Washington Bridge: Cross the bridge and stay on Route 4 West. Proceed to Route 208 North and continue until the highway joins Route 287 South. Take the Skyline Drive Exit (57) and follow above directions.

The Blue Mine Walk, the easiest, takes visitors on a relatively flat, two-mile hike through woods, passing a brook and small waterfall before arriving at the site of two old iron mines.

The second, the High Point Vista/Mine Loop, is a more moderate three-mile hike that takes visitors up to the summit of Wyanokie High Point.

From here the hikes get more rugged. The seven-mile Stream Hopper takes visitors up and down the park's peaks, while Knife's Edge, another seven-mile hike, offers great views, if not terrific footing. These are not for the Sunday walker or faint of heart.

Finally, the Wild Wyanokie Circuit takes visitors on an eight-mile march through—what else?—the park's wild and rugged terrain.

In all of these walks, go prepared. Sturdy hiking boots, insect repellent (in summer), and water bottle are the minimum you should have on you. Bring a backpack and snacks if you're out for a half- or full-day march. It's also a good idea to bring some rain gear and, in warm weather, a sweatshirt in case the weather turns.

Unless you're Daniel Boone and know how to mark trails, carrying a compass along with your trail map is recommended.

Cell phones may or may not work, depending on where you are. If hiking with one or more other people, two-way radios are helpful.

You won't find poison ivy here but you could encounter the occasional black bear prowling about. The New Jersey Department of Fish and Wildlife suggests the following if you see a bear: Don't come within 15 feet of it. If you do have a close-up and personal encounter, don't run or stare the bear in the eyes. Instead, talk calmly and slowly retreat backward.

If you see a bear in the distance, make your presence known. Talk loudly, even clap. If it rises on its haunches, it's just curious and wants a better look at who's strolling through its backyard!

BIRDS

Note: Following are some of the species of you can expect to see throughout the year at Weis. The list is broken down by season for easy reference.

Spring

Blackbirds to Old World Sparrows

Red-Winged Blackbird   Rusty Blackbird

Brown-Headed Cowbird
House Finch
Purple Finch
American Goldfinch

Common Grackle
Northern Oriole
Pine Siskin
House Sparrow

Flycatchers to Vireos

Great-Crested Flycatcher
Least Flycatcher
Eastern Kingbird
Eastern Wood Peewee

Eastern Phoebe
Red-Eyed Vireo
Warbling Vireo
Yellow-Throated Vireo

Jays to Wrens

Black-Capped Chickadee
Brown Creeper
American Crow
Blue Jay
Red-Breasted Nuthatch
White-Breasted Nuthatch
Raven
Bank Swallow
Barn Swallow

Cliff Swallow
Northern Rough-Winged Swallow
Tree Swallow
Chimney Swift
Tufted Titmouse
Carolina Wren
House Wren
Winter Wren

Kinglets to Waxwings

Eastern Bluebird
Gray Catbird
Blue-Gray Gnatcatcher
Gold-Crowned Kinglet
Ruby-Crowned Kinglet
Northern Mockingbird

American Robin
European Starling
Brown Thrasher
Wood Thrush
Veery
Cedar Waxwing

Pigeons to Woodpeckers

Mourning Dove
Northern Flicker
Ruby-Throated Hummingbird

Belted Kingfisher
Common Nighthawk
Yellow-Bellied Sapsucker

Wild Turkey
Whippoorwill
Red-Bellied Woodpecker

Downy Woodpecker
Hairy Woodpecker
Pileated Woodpecker

Raptors

Bald Eagle
Broad-Winged Hawk
Cooper's Hawk
Red-Shouldered Hawk
Red-Tailed Hawk
Sharp-Shinned Hawk

American Kestrel
Barred Owl
Eastern Screech Owl
Great Horned Owl
Northern Saw-Whet Owl

Tanagers to Buntings

Indigo Bunting
Northern Cardinal
Rose-Breasted Grosbeak
Dark-Eyed Junco
Chipping Sparrow
Fox Sparrow
Lincoln's Sparrow

Song Sparrow
Tree Sparrow
White-Crowned Sparrow
White-Throated Sparrow
Scarlet Tanager
Eastern Towhee

Vultures

Black Vulture

Turkey Vulture

Warblers

Blackpoll
Ovenbird
Northern Parula
American Redstart
Bay-Breasted Warbler
Black-and-White Warbler
Black-Throated Blue Warbler
Black-Throated Green Warbler

Blackburnian Warbler
Canada Warbler
Cerulean Warbler
Chestnut-Sided Warbler
Connecticut Warbler
Kentucky Warbler
Magnolia Warbler
Mourning Warbler

Nashville Warbler
Pine Warbler
Prothonotary Warbler
Tennessee Warbler
Worm-Eating Warbler

Yellow Warbler
Yellow-Rumped Warbler
Yellow-Throated Warbler
Louisiana Waterthrush
Northern Waterthrush

Waterfowl

Wood Duck

Mallard

Summer

Blackbirds to Old World Sparrows

Red-Winged Blackbird
Brown-Headed Cowbird
House Finch
Purple Finch

American Goldfinch
Common Grackle
Northern Oriole
House Sparrow

Flycatchers to Vireos

Great-Crested Flycatcher
Least Flycatcher
Eastern Kingbird

Eastern Wood Peewee
Eastern Phoebe
Red-Eyed Vireo

Jays to Wrens

Black-Capped Chickadee
American Crow
Blue Jay
White-Breasted Nuthatch
Barn Swallow

Chimney Swift
Tufted Titmouse
Carolina Wren
House Wren

Kinglets to Waxwings

Eastern Bluebird
Gray Catbird
Blue-Gray Gnatcatcher
Blue Jay
Northern Mockingbird

American Robin
European Starling
Wood Thrush
Veery
Cedar Waxwings

Pigeons to Woodpeckers

Black-Bellied Cuckoo
Yellow-Bellied Cuckoo
Mourning Dove
Northern Flicker
Ruby-Throated Hummingbird
Belted Kingfisher
Common Nighthawk

Wild Turkey
Whippoorwill
Downy Woodpecker
Hairy Woodpecker
Pileated Woodpecker
Red-Bellied Woodpecker

Raptors

Broad-Winged Hawk
Red-Shouldered Hawk
Red-Tailed Hawk

Barred Owl
Eastern Screech Owl
Great Horned Owl

Tanagers to Buntings

Northern Cardinal
Rose-Breasted Grosbeak
Chipping Sparrow
Field Sparrow

Song Sparrow
Scarlet Tanager
Eastern Towhee

Vultures

Black Vulture

Turkey Vulture

Waterfowl

Canada Goose

Warblers

Ovenbird
American Redstart
Black-and-White Warbler
Blue-Winged Warbler

Worm-Eating Warbler
Louisiana Waterthrush
Northern Waterthrush
Common Yellowthroat

Autumn

Blackbirds and Old World Sparrows

Red-Winged Blackbird
Rusty Blackbird
Purple-Headed Cowbird
House Finch
Purple Finch

American Goldfinch
Common Grackle
Northern Oriole
House Sparrow

Flycatchers to Vireos

Great-Crested Flycatcher
Least Flycatcher
Eastern Kingbird

Eastern Wood Peewee
Eastern Phoebe

Jays to Wrens

Black-Capped Chickadee
Brown Creeper
American Crow
Blue Jay
Red-Breasted Nuthatch
White-Breasted Nuthatch

Raven
Barn Swallow
Cliff Swallow
Northern Rough-Winged Swallow
Tree Swallow
Chimney Swift

Tufted Titmouse

Carolina Wren

House Wren

Winter Wren

Kinglets to Waxwings

Eastern Bluebird

Catbird

Blue-Gray Gnatcatcher

Golden-Crowned Kinglet

Ruby-Crowned Kinglet

Northern Mockingbird

American Robin

European Starling

Brown Thrasher

Hermit Thrush

Swainson's Thrush

Wood Thrush

Cedar Waxwing

Pigeons to Woodpeckers

Mourning Dove

Northern Flicker

Ruby-Throated Hummingbird

Belted Kingfisher

Common Nighthawk

Yellow-Bellied Sapsucker

Wild Turkey

Whippoorwill

Downy Woodpecker

Hairy Woodpecker

Pileated Woodpecker

Red-Bellied Woodpecker

Raptors

Bald Eagle

Broad-Winged Hawk

Cooper's Hawk

Red-Shouldered Hawk

Red-Tailed Hawk

Sharp-Shinned Hawk

American Kestrel

Barred Owl

Eastern Screech Owl

Great Horned Owl

Northern Saw-Whet Owl

Tanagers to Buntings

Indigo Bunting

Northern Cardinal

Rose-Breasted Grosbeak

Dark-Eyed Junco

Chipping Sparrow

Field Sparrow

Song Sparrow

White-Throated Sparrow

Scarlet Tanager

Tufted Titmouse

Eastern Towhee

Vultures

Black Vulture   Turkey Vulture

Warblers

Blackpoll   Kentucky Warbler
Ovenbird   Magnolia Warbler
Northern Parula   Mourning Warbler
American Redstart   Nashville Warbler
Bay-Breasted Warbler   Pine Warbler
Black-and-White Warbler   Prothonotary Warbler
Black-Throated Blue Warbler   Tennessee Warbler
Black-Throated Green Warbler   Worm-Eating Warbler
Blackburnian Warbler   Yellow Warbler
Blue-Green Warbler   Yellow-Rumped Warbler
Canada Warbler   Yellow-Throated Warbler
Cerulean Warbler   Louisiana Waterthrush
Chestnut-Sided Warbler   Northern Waterthrush
Connecticut Warbler

Waterfowl

Wood Duck   Mallard

Winter

Blackbirds to Old World Sparrows

Red Crossbill   Evening Grosbeak
White-Winged Crossbill   Redpolls
House Finch   Pine Siskin
Purple Finch

Margaret E. Heggan Free Public Library
208 East Holly Avenue
Hurffville, New Jersey 08080

Jays to Wrens

Black-Capped Chickadee
Brown Creeper
American Crow
Blue Jay
Red-Breasted Nuthatch

White-Breasted Nuthatch
Raven
Carolina Wren
Winter Wren

Kinglets to Waxwings

Golden-Crowned Kinglet
Ruby-Crowned Kinglet

American Robin
Cedar Waxwing

Pigeons to Woodpeckers

Yellow-Bellied Sapsucker
Wild Turkey
Downy Woodpecker

Hairy Woodpecker
Pileated Woodpecker
Red-Bellied Woodpecker

Raptors

Bald Eagle
Cooper's Hawk
Red-Tailed Hawk
Sharp-Shinned Hawk

Barred Owl
Eastern Screech Owl
Great Horned Owl
Northern Saw-Whet Owl

Tanagers to Buntings

Northern Cardinal
Dark-Eyed Junco
Fox Sparrow

Tree Sparrow
Chipping Sparrow
White-Throated Sparrow

Vultures

Black Vulture

Turkey Vulture

Margaret E. Heggan Free Public Library
206 East Holly Avenue
Hurffville, New Jersey 08080

Waterfowl

Wood Duck

Mallard

BUTTERFLIES

Note: The best time to see butterflies is June through August, with the peak season during the first two weeks in July. The best places to see butterflies on the property are in the front area of the visitor's center and the butterfly garden on the trail.

Swallowtails

American Copper
Orange Sulphur
Black Swallowtail

Eastern Tiger Swallowtail
Spicebush Swallowtail
Cabbage White

Hairstreaks

Spring Azure
Baltimore
Eastern Tailed Blue

Banded Hairstreak
Gray Hairstreak
Striped Hairstreak

Fritillaries

Red Admiral
Common Buckeye
Mourning Cloak
Southern Cloudywing
Pearl Crescent
Wild Indigo Duskywing
Hackberry Emperor
Tawny Emperor
Northern Pearly Eye

Great Spangled Fritillary
Meadow Fritillary
American Lady
Painted Lady
Monarch
Common Wood Nymph
Red-Spotted Purple
Little Wood Satyr
Compton Tortoiseshell

Skippers

Northern Broken Dash
Little Glassywing
Delaware Skipper
European Skipper
Hobomok Skipper

Least Skipper
Peck's Skipper
Silver-Spotted Skipper
Zabulon Skipper

MAMMALS

Big Brown Bat
Little Brown Bat
Black Bear
Bobcat
Eastern Chipmunk
Eastern Cottontail
Coyote
White-Tailed Deer
Gray Fox
Red Fox
White-Footed Mouse
Virginia Opossum
Raccoon
Striped Skunk
Shrew
Flying Squirrel
Gray Squirrel
Red Squirrel

Chipmunk

Meadow Vole
Star-Nosed Vole
Woodchuck

REPTILES AND AMPHIBIANS

Salamanders

Red-Spotted Newt
Blue-Spotted Salamander
Marbled Salamander
Northern Red Salamander

Northern Slimy Salamander
Redback Salamander
Spotted Salamander

Snakes

Northern Copperhead
Northern Black Racer
Northern Ringneck
Black Rat Snake
Corn Snake

Eastern Hognose Snake
Eastern Milk Snake
Eastern Ribbon Snake
Northern Water Snake

Turtles

Eastern Box Turtle
Snapping Turtle

Wood Turtle

Frogs

Bull Frog
Green Frog
Northern Gray Tree Frog
Northern Jersey Chorus Frog
Pickerel Frog

Southern Leopard Frog
Wood Frog
Northern Springer Peeper
American Toad
Fowler's Toad

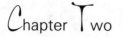

Chapter Two

Lorrimer Sanctuary: Rural 18th-Century Delight in the 21st Century

HISTORY

Wedged into a comfortable grassy nook in the Ramapo Mountain foothills of the Highlands, 14-acre Lorrimer Sanctuary is one of the oldest of New Jersey Audubon's properties. The property was deeded to the group by Lucine Lorrimer, a socialite who died in 1956 at the untimely age of 36. At the time, the property, called "Applewood Farms," included the 16-room hall that is today's visitor center, a caretakers' cottage, a residence with portions built before the Revolutionary War, and a ménage of farm animals that included 14 dogs and two goats.

The goats are gone today, but the public can see more than 150 species of birds that pass here throughout the year.

Lorrimer Sanctuary
790 Ewing Avenue
P.O. Box 125
Franklin Lakes, NJ
07417
Phone: (201) 891-2185
E-mail: lorrimer@
njaudubon.org

Hours: Wednesday
through Friday, 9 A.M.
to 5 P.M.; Saturday, 10
A.M. to 5 P.M.;
Sunday, 1 to 5 P.M.
Closed Monday and
Tuesday.

Facilities: Exhibit/
lecture room,
interpretive displays,
hands-on exhibits, gift
shop, bird feeding
station, meeting
rooms. Programs
include birding trips
and children's
educational programs.

Lorrimer Sign

Lorrimer also has the feel of a private retreat and is probably the most charming of the sanctuaries. With its wood and fieldstone exterior, deep purple door, and "welcome visitor" sign, the manor house looks more like an estate house than it does an administration building/gift shop.

The large office room to the right has a fireplace and a collection of stuffed birds ranging from owls to herons. In the back is a meeting/leisure room where birders can watch the backyard bird feeders.

TERRAIN

Lorrimer is situated in a very woodsy but rather flat part of the Highlands in the northern part of the state. Its various

How to Get Here

From North and South: Route 287 to Exit 59 and
208 South. Take the Ewing Avenue exit and turn
right onto Ewing Avenue. Proceed through a blinking light and stop light. Watch for a driveway
shortly after the light on your right.

shrubs and trees offer excellent protection for most indigenous
New Jersey birds, such as downy woodpeckers.

The sanctuary grounds are landscaped with numerous hard-
woods, what I call "backyard brush," and easy footpaths, giving
you the feeling that you're in a neighbor's back yard as opposed
to being out in rugged backwoods. You won't need heavy-duty
hiking boots and a backpack here!

When you're finished strolling the field and woodland trails,
you can perch on the comfortable sofa in the visitor center, con-
veniently parked before a large bay window in front of the bird
feeders.

TRAILS

Three very easy trails loop
around the property through
fields and woods. They are
mostly flat and leisurely, and
ideal for anyone interested in a
leisurely stroll.

At one-third of a mile long,
the Woodland Trail is the
longest trail. It is a narrow path
that loops behind the estate past
various types of trees starting

Visitor's Center

Field Trail

just beyond the visitor center. The trail takes you past several oak trees and conifers, including scotch pines, Austrian pines, larches, and red cedars.

The one-sixth of a mile Field Trail takes walkers through an area flanked by perennial herbs. In the field stands a birdhouse atop a pole: The house is meant for owls like the barn owl. To see if there are any owls in the vicinity look for "wash," rather impressive-sized splashes of excrement that can be seen down the side of the tree where the owl likes to roost. Owls are also prone to regurgitating the indigestible parts of their meals, like fur and bones: These pellets can be found at the base of their resident trees.

Note: The Woodlands Trail has both poison ivy and Virginia creeper. Many uninitiated hikers can't tell the difference. It's best to remember that poison ivy has three leaflets while Virginia creeper has five. Poison ivy also crawls up trees and looks like a fuzzy vine.

Early fall is the ideal time to watch for migrant birds, especially warblers.

Wildflowers

In April and May, watch for woodland wildflowers like jack-in-the-pulpit, Solomon's seal, false Solomon's seal, nodding trillium, bloodroot, common blue violet, dutchman's breeches, spring beauty, and May-apple.

BIRDS

Spring

Blackbirds to Old World Sparrows

Red-Winged Blackbird
Rusty Blackbird
Brown-Headed Cowbird
Boat-Tailed Grackle
Common Grackle
House Finch
Purple Finch

American Goldfinch
Baltimore Oriole
Northern Oriole
Orchard Oriole
Pine Siskin
House Sparrow

Flycatchers to Vireos

Eastern Kingbird
Eastern Wood Peewee
Eastern Phoebe

Red-Eyed Vireo
White-Eyed Vireo
White-Throated Vireo

Jays to Wrens

Black-Capped Chickadee
Brown Creeper
American Crow
Blue Jay
Purple Martin
Red-Breasted Nuthatch

White-Breasted Nuthatch
Barn Swallow
Tufted Titmouse
Carolina Wren
House Wren
Winter Wren

Kinglets to Waxwings

Eastern Bluebird
Gray Catbird
Mockingbird
American Robin

European Starling
Brown Thrasher
Wood Thrush

Pigeons to Woodpeckers

Mourning Dove
Rock Dove
Northern Flicker
Ruby-Throated Hummingbird
Chimney Swift

Wild Turkey
Downy Woodpecker
Hairy Woodpecker
Pileated Woodpecker
Red-Bellied Woodpecker

Raptors

Broad-Winged Hawk
Cooper's Hawk
Red-Shouldered Hawk
Red-Tailed Hawk
Sharp-Shinned Hawk

American Kestrel
Merlin
Barred Owl
Eastern Screech Owl
Great Horned Owl

Vultures

Black Vulture

Turkey Vulture

Warblers

Blackpoll
Ovenbird
Northern Parula
American Redstart
Black-and-White Warbler
Blackburnian Warbler
Blue-Winged Warbler

Cerulean Warbler
Connecticut Warbler
Kentucky Warbler
Louisiana Warbler
Magnolia Warbler
Pine Warbler
Common Yellowthroat

Prothonotary Warbler
Tennessee Warbler
Worm-Eating Warbler
Yellow Warbler

Yellow-Rumped Warbler
Yellow-Throated Warbler
Louisiana Waterthrush
Northern Waterthrush

Waterfowl

Canada Goose

Summer

Blackbirds to Old World Sparrows

Red-Winged Blackbird
Rusty Blackbird
Brown-Headed Cowbird
House Finch

Purple Finch
American Goldfinch
Common Grackle
Northern Oriole

Flycatchers to Vireos

Acadian Flycatcher
Great-Crested Flycatcher
Least Flycatcher
Willow Flycatcher
Yellow-Bellied Flycatcher
Eastern Kingbird

Eastern Wood Peewee
Eastern Phoebe
Red-Eyed Vireo
Warbling Vireo
White-Eyed Vireo
Yellow-Throated Vireo

Jays to Wrens

Black-Capped Chickadee
American Crow
Blue Jay
Purple Martin
Barn Swallow

Chimney Swift
Tufted Titmouse
Carolina Wren
House Wren

Kinglets to Waxwings

Eastern Bluebird
Gray Catbird
Blue-Gray Gnatcatcher
Northern Mockingbird
American Robin

European Starling
Brown Thrasher
Wood Thrush
Veery

Pigeons to Woodpeckers

Black-Bellied Cuckoo
Yellow-Bellied Cuckoo
Mourning Dove
Rock Dove
Northern Flicker
Ruby-Throated Hummingbird

Belted Kingfisher
Wild Turkey
Downy Woodpecker
Hairy Woodpecker
Pileated Woodpecker
Red-Bellied Woodpecker

Raptors

Broad-Winged Hawk
Cooper's Hawk
Red-Shouldered Hawk
Red-Tailed Hawk

American Kestrel
Barred Owl
Eastern Screech Owl
Great Horned Owl

Tanagers to Buntings

Northern Cardinal
Rose-Breasted Grosbeak
Chipping Sparrow
Field Sparrow

Song Sparrow
Scarlet Tanager
Eastern Towhee

Vultures

Black Vulture

Turkey Vulture

Warblers

Ovenbird
American Redstart
Black-and-White Warbler

Blue-Winged Warbler
Common Yellowthroat

Waterfowl

Canada Goose

Autumn

Blackbirds and Old World Sparrows

Red-Winged Blackbird
House Finch
American Goldfinch

Common Grackle
House Sparrow

Pigeons to Woodpeckers

Mourning Dove
Northern Flicker
Ruby-Throated Hummingbird
Common Nighthawk
Yellow-Bellied Sapsucker

Downy Woodpecker
Hairy Woodpecker
Pileated Woodpecker
Red-Bellied Woodpecker

Raptors

Broad-Winged Hawk
Cooper's Hawk
Red-Shouldered Hawk
Red-Tailed Hawk
Sharp-Shinned Hawk
American Kestrel

Merlin
Barred Owl
Eastern Screech Owl
Great Horned Owl
Northern Saw-Whet

Tanagers to Buntings

Northern Cardinal
Rose-Breasted Grosbeak
Dark-Eyed Junco
Chipping Sparrow
Field Sparrow

Song Sparrow
White-Throated Sparrow
Tufted Titmouse
Eastern Towhee

Vultures

Black Vulture

Turkey Vulture

Warblers

Blackpoll
Ovenbird
Northern Parula
American Redstart
Black-and-White Warbler
Black-Throated Blue Warbler
Blackburnian Warbler
Canada Warbler
Cerulean Warbler
Chestnut-Sided Warbler
Connecticut Warbler

Kentucky Warbler
Magnolia Warbler
Mourning Warbler
Prothonotary Warbler
Tennessee Warbler
Worm-Eating Warbler
Yellow-Rumped Warbler
Yellow-Throated Warbler
Northern Waterthrush
Common Yellowthroat

Waterfowl

Wood Duck

Mallard

Blackbirds to Old World Sparrows

House Finch
American Goldfinch

Common Grackle
House Sparrow

Jays to Wrens

Carolina Chickadee
American Crow

Blue Jay
Tufted Titmouse

Kinglets to Waxwings

American Robin
European Starling

Cedar Waxwing

Pigeons to Woodpeckers

Mourning Dove
Northern Flicker
Downy Woodpecker

Hairy Woodpecker
Pileated Woodpecker
Red-Bellied Woodpecker

Raptors

Red-Tailed Hawk
Barred Owl

Eastern Screech Owl
Great Horned Owl

Tanagers to Buntings

Northern Cardinal
Dark-Eyed Junco

Chipping Sparrow
White-Throated Sparrow

Vultures

Black Vulture

Turkey Vulture

Waterfowl

Canada Goose

BUTTERFLIES

Note: The best time to see butterflies is June through August, with the peak season during the first two weeks in July. The best places to see butterflies on the property are either in the parking lot area near the front of the visitor center, or the butterfly garden on the trail.

Fritillaries

Red Admiral
Common Buckeye
Mourning Cloak
Southern Cloudywing
Pearl Crescent
Wild Indigo Duskywing
Hackberry Emperor
Tawny Emperor
Northern Pearly Eye

Great Spangled Fritillary
Meadow Fritillary
American Lady
Painted Lady
Monarch
Common Wood Nymph
Red-Spotted Purple
Little Wood Satyr
Compton Tortoiseshell

Hairstreaks

Spring Azure
Baltimore
Eastern Tailed Blue

Banded Hairstreak
Gray Hairstreak
Striped Hairstreak

Skippers

Northern Broken Dash
Little Glassywing
Delaware Skipper
European Skipper
Hobomok Skipper

Least Skipper
Peck's Skipper
Silver-Spotted Skipper
Zabulon Skipper

Swallowtails

American Copper
Orange Sulphur
Black Swallowtail

Eastern Tiger Swallowtail
Spicebush Swallowtail
Cabbage White

MAMMALS

Big Brown Bat
Red Bat
Eastern Chipmunk
Eastern Cottontail
White-Tailed Deer
White-Footed Mouse

Virginia Opossum
Raccoon
Striped Skunk
Gray Squirrel
Red Squirrel
Woodchuck

REPTILES AND AMPHIBIANS

Salamanders

Blue Salamander

Snakes

Eastern Garter Snake

Milk Snake

FERNS AND WILDFLOWERS

Rue Anemone
Bee Balm
Christmas Fern
Cinnamon Fern
Maiden Hair Fern
Wart Ginseng
False Hellbore

Trout Lily
Milkweed
Rattlesnake Plaintain
Ragweed
Tall Meadow Rue
Black-Eyed Susan
Thistle

TREES AND SHRUBS

Smooth Alder
Southern Arrowwood
White Ash
Quaking Aspen
Early Azaelea
Common Barberry
Japanese Barberry
Basswood
Sweet Bay
Beech
Black Birch
Gray Birch
Yellow Birch
Highbush Blueberry
Strawberry Bush

Butternut
Red Cedar
Black Cherry
Sweet Cherry
American Chestnut
Alternate-Leaved Dogwood
Flowering Dogwood
Panicled Dogwood
Red-Osier Dogwood
Silky Dogwood
Box Elder
Common Elder
American Elm
Slippery Elm
Winged Euonymus

Pinxter Flower	Mockernut
Forsythia	White Mulberry
Sour Gum	Black Oak
Sweet Gum	Chestnut Oak
Black Haw	Pin Oak
American Hazel	Red Oak
Beaked Hazel	White Oak
Witch Hazel	Autumn Olive
Hemlock	Sweet Pepperbush
Butternut Hickory	Common Privet
Pignut Hickory	Sassafras
Shagbark Hickory	Spicebush
American Holly	Norway Spruce
Hop Hornbeam	Smooth Sumac
Ironwood	Staghorn Sumac
Poison Ivy	Biltmore Thorn
Oblongleaf Juneberry	Tulip Tree
Lilac	Cranberry Viburnum
Black Locust	Maple-Leaved Viburnum
Honey Locust	Black Walnut
Red Maple	Pussy Willow
Sugar Maple	Winterberry

Chapter Three

Scherman-Hoffman
Wildlife Sanctuary:
Warblers and Wonderwalks

HISTORY

The 260 acres of the Scherman-Hoffman Wildlife Sanctuary incorporate two adjacent properties, a 125-acre tract donated by Henry and Doris Scherman in 1965, and a 135-acre property donated in two separate parcels by beverage magnate G. Frederick Hoffman in 1973 and 1975.

How both came to fall into the hands of New Jersey Audubon are good examples of how "normal" people—that is, nonbirders—grow compelled to deed their properties to the higher cause of environmental education and preservation.

As the story goes, the Schermans were visiting Lorrimer Sanctuary one day, when Henry Scherman suddenly asked, "How do you go about setting up something like this?" Actually, Henry had a friend by the

Scherman-Hoffman Wildlife Sanctuary

11 Hardscrabble Rd.
Bernardsville, NJ 07924

Phone: (908) 766-5787

E-mail: scherman-hoffman@njaudubon.org

Hours: Tuesday through Saturday, 9 A.M. to 5 P.M. Sunday, noon to 5 P.M. Closed Mondays and Holidays. Trails open daily to 5 P.M.

Facilities: Book and gift store, special events room for art/photography exhibits, the Mary Kay Roach Memorial Bird Room, and the Edith Gambrill Memorial Research Library. Also the headquarters of NJAS, located at 9 Hardscrabble Road.

Note: Scherman-Hoffman expanded its nature center facilities in 2003. The expansion includes a second-story observation platform, new classrooms, and wheelchair accessibility.

The Hoffman Building

name of Richard Pough, who just happened to be one of the founders of the Nature Conservancy, so he knew a little bit about the need for conservation. And, he had been looking for a good cause he could donate his property to.

The rest is history. Scherman gave the property to New Jersey Audubon, and Scherman Sanctuary opened in 1966. The sanctuaries were merged in 1973.

How to Get Here

From the North: Take Route 287 South to Exit 30B. Bear right off the ramp and proceed to the light at the intersection of Route 202. Go straight through the light onto Childs Road. Bear right on Hardscrabble Road and proceed for about a mile until you see the sign. Turn right onto the paved road and proceed up the hill to the Hoffman Building, where you can park. To access the Scherman parking lot, continue on Hardscrabble Road until you see it on your left.

From the South: Take 287 North to Exit 30A. Bear right over the overpass and proceed to the light at the intersection of Route 202. Follow above directions.

From New York: From the George Washington Bridge, take Route 95 to Route 80 West. Continue on to Route 287 and follow above directions. Take Route 287 South. Follow above directions. From the Lincoln Tunnel, take Route 3 West to Route 46 West to Route 80 West. Continue on to Route 287 and follow directions above.

TERRAIN

Situated in the north central part of the state, Scherman-Hoffman is wedged between the floodplains of the headwaters of the Passaic River, the second longest river in New Jersey (the Raritan River being the first), and the foothills of the state's Highlands region. The ecological variations provide numerous types of birding and hiking opportunities, all of which can be appreciated during half-day or full-day hikes, or on any one of the nature walks offered by Scherman-Hoffman naturalists.

Birders on the Field Loop

Birding opportunities abound at Scherman-Hoffman, especially in the spring and fall, when birds are migrating to their summer and winter habitats.

According to New Jersey Audubon, more than 175 of the more than 400 birds that frequent the state have been sighted here, including up to 25 species of warblers, tiny songbirds with magnificent, melodic voices. The 60-plus species of birds that nest here include worm-eating and cerulean warblers, Eastern bluebirds, pileated woodpeckers, black-capped chickadees, yellow-shafted flickers, red-bellied woodpeckers, wild turkeys, and great-horned and Eastern screech owls.

Sanctuary Sign

Rarities occur. In May 2001, during the World Series of Birding, the group I was birding with first heard, then spotted, a Sandhill Crane in flight over the Scherman trails.

TRAILS

Scherman-Hoffman's trail circuit meanders along three miles of paths that range from an easy ramble on flat ground to a moderate uphill hike. Each path represents the diversity of the area's geographical characteristics, from flatlands and fields to wetlands and woods.

There are three main trails: The Field Loop, the Dogwood Trail, and the River Trail. Embedded in these trails are numbered stakes that point to various flora and fauna of interest. A guide to these points is available at the visitor center for $1.00.

THE FIELD LOOP

The Field Loop takes you on a leisurely stroll through butterfly fields and meadows filled with indigenous wildflowers, including witch hazel, bee balm, milkweed, black-eyed susan, and tall meadow rue.

The best place to start on the loop is in the parking lot of the Hoffman Building. Walk down to the sign and turn right onto the trail, passing several apple trees. As you walk toward the woods you'll pass patches of milkweed and dogbane. In June and July, the fields are resplendent with butterflies, including eastern tiger, black and spicebush swallowtails, cabbage whites, banded hairstreaks, great spangled and meadow fritillaries, mourning cloaks, American and painted ladies, little wood satyrs, silver-spotted-skippers, and others.

The trail takes you on a path between the woods and the fields, or the "edge" area bordering the field and forest. Here you just might see eastern towhees kicking up ground cover in search of food while a rare wood turtle crawls by, or a garter snake takes advantage of the warm sun shining on the trail. Edges are also marked off by a variety of vine-type bushes, like viburnum and wineberry, whose berries offer many thrushes and songbirds a nifty, if not colorful meal.

Bluebird and wren boxes pepper the fields and are well used, if not by the birds for which they're intended, then by tree swallows, whose blue backs glow iridescent in the sunlight, offering terrific photo opportunities. If you're lucky, you might also catch a glimpse of red and gray foxes, white-tailed deer, and even the elusive mink. The Field Loop is also an excellent place to watch for colorful, raccoon-eyed cedar waxwings, especially in June, when the birds cluster around the mulberry trees, nipping the berries.

The Field Loop gradually passes through two fields before sloping up again toward the driveway leading back to the Hoffman Building. If you wish, take a short loop around the upper field, where you will see black and gray birch trees and flowering dogwood. Other trees in the area include mockernut, shagbark hickories, white ash, popular, and others.

The area where the loop reconnects to the Field Loop is a good place to see blue-winged and yellow warblers in the spring.

The River Trail

The River Trail, the shortest trail on the grounds, takes hikers along the banks of the Passaic River headwaters before sloping up to meet the Dogwood Trail. At this point, the Passaic is no more than a babbling brook, hardly suggestive of the 60-foot breadth it will take miles downriver before its waters race over the 70-foot drop of the Great Falls in the city of Paterson.

On the River Trail, hikers can catch a glimpse of the elusive wood duck, a beautiful albeit elusive duck that roosts in trees. How can a duck roost in a tree? Contrary to rumors, it's not with Velcro. Wood ducks have a talon on their webbed feet that allows them to dig into bark for balance. Also look out for Louisiana waterthrushes and winter wrens.

Red efts and northern red salamanders also call the head-waters home, as do two-lined, spotted, slimy, red-backed, and dusky salamanders. Ferns abound in this habitat, including the Christmas and maiden hair varieties.

THE DOGWOOD TRAIL

The Dogwood Trail winds its way from the bottom of the parking lot of the New Jersey Audubon headquarters offices up into the sanctuary woods. It's here that you'll hear—and see, if your eyesight is keen and the foliage isn't too dense—flickers, eastern towhees, warblers, pileated and red-bellied woodpeckers, veerys (thrushes known for their haunting duo-toned song), and wood thrushes.

Be careful not to step on the tree frogs that blend brilliantly with fallen leaves. The same goes for the eastern garter snakes, which like to bask under leaves and other ground cover when the weather is warm enough.

Although not severely steep, this trail can be challenging for those who tire easily, so take your time as you climb. Pause and enjoy the woods around you.

If you can, take one of the many night hikes Scherman-Hoffman naturalists host year-round. Hikes are scheduled for the week of the full moon, and participants walk without flashlights. The objective of these hikes is to listen for owls and to simply enjoy the trails in moonlight.

If you've never been on a night hike, I suggest you go. The woods will never seem the same again.

Robin in the Birdbath

BIRDS

Bitterns to Vultures

Great Blue Heron
Green Heron

Black Vulture
Turkey Vulture

Blackbirds to Old World Sparrows

Red-Winged Blackbird
Rusty Blackbird
Brown-Headed Cowbird
House Finch
Purple Finch
American Goldfinch
Boat-Tailed Grackle

Common Grackle
Baltimore Oriole
Northern Oriole
Orchard Oriole
Pine Siskin
House Sparrow

Flycatchers to Vireos

Acadian Flycatcher
Least Flycatcher
Olive-Sided Flycatcher
Willow Flycatcher
Yellow-Bellied Flycatcher
Eastern Wood Peewee

Eastern Phoebe
Eastern Kingbird
Red-Eyed Vireo
White-Eyed Vireo
White-Throated Vireo

Jays to Wrens

Black-Capped Chickadee
Brown Creeper
American Crow
Fish Crow
Blue Jay
Purple Martin

Bank Swallow
Barn Swallow
Rough-Winged Swallow
Tree Swallow
Tufted Titmouse
Red-Breasted Nuthatch

White-Breasted Nuthatch
Carolina Wren

House Wren
Winter Wren

Kinglets to Waxwings

Eastern Bluebird
Gray Catbird
Blue-Gray Gnatcatcher
Golden-Crowned Kinglet
Ruby-Crowned Kinglet
Mockingbird
American Robin
European Starling
Brown Thrasher
Gray-Cheeked Thrush

Hermit Thrush
Swainson's Thrush
Wood Thrush
Veery
Red-Eyed Vireo
Solitary Vireo
Warbling Vireo
White-Eyed Vireo
Yellow-Breasted Vireo
Cedar Waxwing

Pigeons to Woodpeckers

Mourning Dove
Rock Dove
Northern Flicker
Roughed Grouse
Ruby-Throated Hummingbird
Belted Kingfisher
Common Nighthawk
Yellow-Bellied Sapsucker

Chimney Swift
Wild Turkey
American Woodcock
Downy Woodpecker
Hairy Woodpecker
Pileated Woodpecker
Red-Bellied Woodpecker

Raptors

Northern Harrier
Broad-Winged Hawk
Cooper's Hawk
Red-Shouldered Hawk
Red-Tailed Hawk
Sharp-Shinned Hawk

American Kestrel
Merlin
Osprey
Barred Owl
Eastern Screech Owl
Great Horned Owl

Tanagers to Buntings

Indigo Bunting
Northern Cardinal
Evening Grosbeak
Rose-Breasted Grosbeak
Dark-Eyed Junco
Chipping Sparrow
Field Sparrow

Fox Sparrow
Lincoln's Sparrow
Song Sparrow
Tree Sparrow
White-Throated Sparrow
Scarlet Tanager
Eastern Towhee

Warblers

Blackpoll
Ovenbird
Northern Parula
American Restart
Common Yellow Throat
Black-and-White Warbler
Blackburnian Warbler
Blue-Winged Warbler
Cape May Warbler
Cerulean Warbler
Connecticut Warbler
Kentucky Warbler

Louisiana Warbler
Magnolia Warbler
Pine Warbler
Prothonotary Warbler
Tennessee Warbler
Worm-Eating Warbler
Yellow Warbler
Yellow-Rumped Warbler
Yellow-Throated Warbler
Louisiana Waterthrush
Northern Waterthrush

Waterfowl

American Black Duck
Wood Duck

Canada Goose
Mallard

Summer

Bitterns to Vultures

Great Blue Heron
Green Heron

Black Vulture
Turkey Vulture

Blackbirds to Old World Sparrows

Red-Winged Blackbird
Rusty Blackbird
Brown-Headed Cowbird
House Finch

Purple Finch
American Goldfinch
Common Grackle
Northern Oriole

Flycatchers to Vireos

Acadian Flycatcher
Great-Crested Flycatcher
Least Flycatcher
Willow Flycatcher
Yellow-Bellied Flycatcher
Eastern Kingbird

Eastern Wood Peewee
Eastern Phoebe
Red-Eyed Vireo
Warbling Vireo
White-Eyed Vireo
Yellow-Throated Vireo

Jays to Wrens

Black-Capped Chickadee
Brown Creeper
American Crow
Fish Crow
Blue Jay
Purple Martin
Bank Swallow

Barn Swallow
Rough-Winged Swallow
Tree Swallow
Chimney Swift
Tufted Titmouse
Carolina Wren
House Wren

Kinglets to Waxwings

Eastern Bluebird
Gray Catbird
Blue-Gray Gnatcatcher
Northern Mockingbird
American Robin

European Starling
Brown Thrasher
Wood Thrush
Veery
Cedar Waxwing

Pigeons to Woodpeckers

Black-Bellied Cuckoo
Yellow-Bellied Cuckoo
Mourning Dove
Rock Dove
Northern Flicker
Roughed Grouse
Ruby-Throated Hummingbird
Belted Kingfisher

Common Nighthawk
Wild Turkey
American Woodcock
Downy Woodpecker
Hairy Woodpecker
Pileated Woodpecker
Red-Bellied Woodpecker

Raptors

Broad-Winged Hawk
Cooper's Hawk
Red-Shouldered Hawk
Red-Tailed Hawk

American Kestrel
Barred Owl
Eastern Screech Owl
Great Horned Owl

Tanagers to Buntings

Northern Cardinal
Rose-Breasted Grosbeak
Chipping Sparrow
Field Sparrow

Song Sparrow
Scarlet Tanager
Eastern Towhee

Warblers

Ovenbird
American Redstart
Common Yellow Throat

Black-and-White Warbler
Blue-Winged Warbler

Waterfowl

Wood Duck
Canada Goose

Mallard

Bitterns to Vultures

Great Blue Heron
Black Vulture

Turkey Vulture

Blackbirds and Old World Sparrows

Red-Winged Blackbird
House Finch
American Goldfinch

Common Grackle
House Sparrow

Pigeons to Woodpeckers

Mourning Dove
Northern Flicker
Ruby-Throated Hummingbird
Common Nighthawk
Yellow-Bellied Sapsucker

Downy Woodpecker
Hairy Woodpecker
Pileated Woodpecker
Red-Bellied Woodpecker

Raptors

Northern Harrier
Broad-Winged Hawk
Cooper's Hawk
Red-Shouldered Hawk
Red-Tailed Hawk
Sharp-Shinned Hawk
American Kestrel

Merlin
Osprey
Barred Owl
Eastern Screech Owl
Great Horned Owl
Northern Saw Whet

Tanagers to Buntings

Northern Cardinal
Rose-Breasted Grosbeak

Dark-Eyed Junco
Chipping Sparrow

Field Sparrow
Song Sparrow
White-Throated Sparrow

Tufted Titmouse
Eastern Towhee

Warblers

Blackpoll
Ovenbird
Northern Parula
American Redstart
Black-and-White Warbler
Black-Throated Blue Warbler
Blackburnian Warbler
Canada Warbler
Cerulean Warbler
Chestnut-Sided Warbler
Connecticut Warbler

Kentucky Warbler
Magnolia Warbler
Mourning Warbler
Prothonotary Warbler
Tennessee Warbler
Worm-Eating Warbler
Yellow-Rumped Warbler
Yellow-Throated Warbler
Northern Waterthrush
Common Yellowthroat

Waterfowl

Wood Duck

Mallard

Winter

Bitterns to Vultures

Great Blue Heron
Black Vulture

Turkey Vulture

Blackbirds to Old World Sparrow

House Finch
American Goldfinch

Common Grackle
House Sparrow

Jays to Wrens

Carolina Chickadee

American Crow

Blue Jay

Tufted Titmouse

Kinglets to Waxwings

American Robin

European Starling

Cedar Waxwing

Pigeons to Woodpeckers

Mourning Dove

Northern Flicker

Downy Woodpecker

Hairy Woodpecker

Pileated Woodpecker

Red-Bellied Woodpecker

Raptors

Red-Tailed Hawk

Barred Owl

Eastern Screech Owl

Great Horned Owl

Tanagers to Buntings

Northern Cardinal

Dark-Eyed Junco

Chipping Sparrow

White-Throated Sparrow

Waterfowl

Wood Duck

Mallard

BUTTERFLIES

Note: The best time to see butterflies at Scherman-Hoffman is anywhere between June and August, with the peak season during the first two weeks in July. The best places to see butterflies on the property are the lower butterfly field just behind the New Jersey Audubon headquarter offices, 9 Hardscrabble Road, and in the "deer-proof" butterfly/wildflower garden across from the entrance to the Hoffman Building at 11 Hardscrabble Road.

Fritillaries

Red Admiral
Common Buckeye
Mourning Cloak
Southern Cloudywing
Pearl Crescent
Wild Indigo Duskywing
Hackberry Emperor
Tawny Emperor
Northern Pearly Eye

Great Spangled Fritillary
Meadow Fritillary
American Lady
Painted Lady
Monarch
Common Wood Nymph
Red-Spotted Purple
Little Wood Satyr
Compton Tortoiseshell

Hairstreaks

Spring Azure
Baltimore
Eastern Tailed Blue

Banded Hairstreak
Gray Hairstreak
Striped Hairstreak

Skippers

Northern Broken Dash
Little Glassywing
Delaware Skipper
European Skipper
Hobomok Skipper

Least Skipper
Peck's Skipper
Silver-Spotted Skipper
Zabulon Skipper

Swallowtails

American Copper
Orange Sulphur
Black Swallowtail

Eastern Tiger Swallowtail
Spicebush Swallowtail
Cabbage White

MAMMALS

Big Brown Bat
Red Bat
Eastern Chipmunk
Eastern Cottontail
White-Tailed Deer
Gray Fox
Red Fox
Mink
Eastern Mole
White-Footed Mouse
Muskrat
Little Brown Myotis

Virginia Opossum
Raccoon
Norway Rat
Masked Shrew
N. Short-Tailed Shrew
Striped Skunk
Gray Squirrel
Red Squirrel
S. Flying Squirrel
Meadow Vole
Long-Tailed Weasel
Woodchuck

REPTILES AND AMPHIBIANS

Salamanders

Red Eft
Dusky Salamander
Northern Red Salamander
Red-Backed Salamander

Slimy Salamander
Spotted Salamander
Two-Lined Salamander

Snakes

Northern Black Racer

Eastern Garter Snake

E. Ribbon Snake
Milk Snake
Northern Brown (DeKay's) Snake

Ringneck Snake
Northern Watersnake

Turtles

Box Turtle
Painted Turtle

Snapping Turtle
Wood Turtle (endangered)

FERNS AND WILDFLOWERS

Rue Anemone
Bee Balm
Christmas Fern
Cinnamon Fern
Maiden Hair Fern
Wart Ginseng
False Hellbore

Trout Lily
Milkweed
Rattlesnake Plaintain
Ragweed
Tall Meadow Rue
Black-Eyed Susan
Thistle

TREES AND SHRUBS

Smooth Alder
Southern Arrowwood
White Ash
Quaking Aspen
Early Azaelea
Common Barberry
Japanese Barberry
Basswood
Sweet Bay
Beech
Black Birch

Gray Birch
Yellow Birch
Highbush Blueberry
Strawberry Bush
Butternut
Red Cedar
Black Cherry
Sweet Cherry
American Chestnut
Alternate-Leaved Dogwood
Flowering Dogwood

Panicled Dogwood	Black Locust
Red-Osier Dogwood	Honey Locust
Silky Dogwood	Red Maple
Box Elder	Sugar Maple
Common Elder	Mockernut
American Elm	White Mulberry
Slippery Elm	Black Oak
Winged Euonymus	Chestnut Oak
Pinxter Flower	Pin Oak
Forsythia	Red Oak
Sour Gum	White Oak
Sweet Gum	Autumn Olive
Black Haw	Sweet Pepperbush
American Hazel	Common Privet
Beaked Hazel	Sassafras
Witch Hazel	Spicebush
Hemlock	Norway Spruce
Butternut Hickory	Smooth Sumac
Pignut Hickory	Staghorn Sumac
Shagbark Hickory	Biltmore Thorn
American Holly	Tulip Tree
Hop Hornbeam	Cranberry Viburnum
Ironwood	Maple-Leaved Viburnum
Poison Ivy	Black Walnut
Oblongleaf Juneberry	Pussy Willow
Lilac	Winterberry

Chapter Four

Sandy Hook Bird Observatory:
Cape May of the North

HISTORY

The Sandy Hook Bird Observatory is one of New Jersey Audubon's newest staffed nature centers, its director and staff having moved from the Owl Haven center in Monmouth County at the beginning of 2002. The new center sits on "Officer's Row" in historic Fort Hancock in the National Gateway Recreation Area, near the tip of the six-mile-long peninsula in what was once the Stewards' Building.

The center is situated in a colorful part of New Jersey. Sandy Hook Channel sits at the entrance of New York Harbor and has been used as the primary entrance for ships since the 17th century.

Sandy Hook's lighthouse, built in 1764, is one of the oldest working lighthouses in the country, maintained by

Sandy Hook Bird Observatory

20 Hartshorne Drive
Fort Hancock, NJ
07732

Phone: (732) 872-2500

E-mail:
shbo@njaudubon.org

Hours: Tuesday
through Saturday,
10 A.M. to 5 P.M.;
Sunday, 1 to 5 P.M.

Facilities: Book and
gift store, museum.

Spermaceti Cove Visitor's Center,
National Park Service

the U.S. Coast Guard from its station at the northern most point of the peninsula.

The infamous buccaneer Captain Kidd is said to have buried loot here, and from the War of 1812 until the mid-1970s, the area was used as a strategic army post, with numerous fortifications erected over the decades. The last fortification, named Fort Hancock after Civil War Union General Winfield Scott Hancock, was established in 1895. It was used as a training center during World War I, and was later a staging area for troops bound for the European Theater during World War II. During the Cold War it housed Nike Ajax Missiles, ready to defend the metropolitan area.

The Fort was deactivated in 1974 and turned over to the National Park Service. Today, Sandy Hook is one of the most popular getaway spots in the greater New York area. Its four beaches are filled to capacity on summer weekends, while the rest of the year the 1,665-acre barrier beach is home to windsurfers, joggers, fishermen, bikers, and, yes, birders and walkers.

How to Get Here

From the North: Take Route 287 South or the New Jersey Turnpike to the Garden State Parkway. Proceed south to Exit 117 (NOT Exit 117A). Follow the exit ramp to Route 36 and proceed south for about 11 miles. Signs will point to Gateway National Recreation Park.

Once inside the park, go straight down Hartshorne Drive. Guardian Park, with its white Nike missile memorial, will be in front of the center.

The National Park Service charges for the use of beaches from mid-June to Labor Day. Sandy Hook has no summer entrance fee for birding as long as you park in designated lots. Tell the toll attendant you are birding and not parking in beach access lots. This allows you to park at the Visitor Center, Horseshoe Cove, Scout Camp, all Fort Hancock lots, and SHBO. Fees are not charged before 7:00 A.M. and after 5:00 P.M.

Bring typical New Jersey birding gear: warm, layered clothes for the colder months, insect repellent for the warmer months. Poison ivy—what I call New Jersey kudzu—is abundant on Sandy Hook all year. Be observant and carry a preventative like Tecnu, just in case.

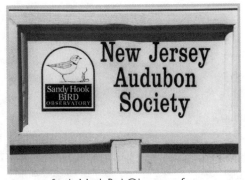

Sandy Hook Bird Observatory Sign

TERRAIN

Sandy Hook isn't called Sandy Hook for nothing. Poised on the threshold to the Atlantic, it exemplifies the qualities of New Jersey's Outer Coastal Plain. On one hand, it's throat-dry arid, an environment that best suits what I think should be adopted as the official state shrub, poison ivy. On the other hand, its tidal wetlands are excellent havens for shorebirds like willets, and for typical wetland and marsh species like egrets and herons. Sora and bitterns have also been known to take up residence in its freshwater phragmites wetlands.

TRAILS

The Sandy Hook Bird Observatory has been informally called "Cape May of the North" both for the amount of species (more than 330) attracted to its location, and for the staff's commitment to educating visitors on wildlife conservation and the environment.

The peninsula offers numerous trails. Because of its length, it's best to drive to a specific area and walk.

Be advised that several of these trails are packed with poison ivy. Trails are either over boardwalks or sandy paths. Most of the trails are flat with the exception of the dunes near the hawk-watch platform.

Sandy Hook Beaches Are Excellent Birding Spots

Sandy Hook is a treat to walk any time of the year, but if you're interested in birding, then the best times to bird are during the spring and fall migrations, when warblers and raptors fill the skies; and in winter, when a multitude of waterfowl seek harbor in its protected coves on the west side. In December 2000, a snowy owl took up residence in the south beach area while waiting for its own arctic tundra to thaw.

Although Sandy Hook is far smaller in area than Cape May, its birding diversity makes it tough to decide where to start. My personal preference is to start near the Spermaceti Cove Visitor Center and drive up to Gunnison and North beaches.

In spring, you can check out the dunes outside the center entrance. In late fall or winter, head across the road to Spermaceti Cove, where a boardwalk takes you to the observation area overlooking the cove. (A spotting scope is suggested for looking out across the inlet.) Very often you can find an assortment of waterfowl here, from hooded mergansers

Song Sparrow

to ring-necked ducks, blue-winged teal, and American black ducks. Bitterns, clapper rails, herons, and egrets can also be found in the marshes fronting the water. In spring check out the osprey platforms for nests.

Also be sure to take a good look at one of the area's few intact holly forests. The roots of holly trees are so sensitive that the park keeps this section closed to frequent tromping. Visiting the forest is only done through a scheduled hike. You can also view beautiful maritime forest along the south beach dune trail.

From here, you can drive down Hartshorne Drive to North Beach and the Sandy Hook Migration Watch observation platform. The deck looks out across the Atlantic Ocean, and from here you can catch a spectacular view of the New York City skyline.

In spring and fall, it's also a good idea to stop at Gunnison Beach near the old ordnance testing site and North Pond to look for warblers along the trails. More than 20 types of warblers can be found here. Watch the species closely in the fall: between immature warblers and adults molting into winter coat, identifying them can be confusing. They're not called "CFWs"—Confusing Fall Warblers—for nothing!

A small warning about North Beach: Like Cape May's Higbee's Beach, Gunnison Beach has been a notorious summer hangout for nude beachgoers since the dawn of time. Unless you're seeking birds of another feather, you may care to avoid this area.

Veery

Leaving Sandy Hook, I prefer to drive down Hartshorne Drive and stop at the parking area for Horseshoe Cove.

BIRDS

Spring

Flycatchers, Swallows, Jays, and Crows

Fish Crow	Eastern Kingbird
Blue Jay	Eastern Wood Pewee

Geese and Ducks

Brant
Bufflehead
Canvasback
American Black Duck
Ruddy Duck
Common Goldeneye
Canada Goose
Snow Goose
Mallard

Red-Breasted Merganser
Oldsquaw
Lesser Scaup
Black Scoter
Surf Scoter
White-Winged Scoter
Blue-Winged Teal
Green-Winged Teal

Grebes

Double-Crested Cormorant
Great Cormorant

Northern Gannet

Grosbeaks, Finches, and Sparrows

Indigo Bunting
Northern Cardinal
House Finch
Purple Finch
American Goldfinch
Evening Grosbeak
Rose-Breasted Grosbeak
Dark-Eyed Junco

American Tree Sparrow
Chipping Sparrow
Field Sparrow
Fox Sparrow
Savannah Sparrow
Swamp Sparrow
Vesper Sparrow

Herons, Egrets, and Bitterns

American Bittern
Cattle Egret
Great Egret
Snowy Egret
Black-Crowned Night Heron

Great Blue Heron
Green Heron
Little Blue Heron
Tricolored Heron
Yellow-Crowned Night Heron

Kingfishers

Belted Kingfisher

Loons

Common Loon

Red-Throated Loon

Pigeons to Woodpeckers

Mourning Dove
Rock Dove

Ruby-Throated Hummingbird

Plovers, Sandpipers, Gulls, and Terns

Dunlin
Bonaparte's Gull
Great Black-Backed Gull
Laughing Gull
Ring-Billed Gull
Killdeer
Red Knot
Black-Bellied Plover
Piping Plover
Semipalmated Plover
Sanderling

Least Sandpiper
Black Skimmer
Wilson's Snipe
Common Tern
Least Tern
Ruddy Turnstone
Willet
American Woodcock
Greater Yellowlegs
Lesser Yellowlegs

Rails and Coots

American Coot
Clapper Rail

Virginia Rail

Titmice, Nuthatches, Wrens, and Mimic Thrushes

Gray Catbird
Black-Capped Chickadee

Brown Creeper
Northern Mockingbird

American Robin
Brown Thrasher

House Wren
Winter Wren

Vultures, Hawks, Osprey, and Falcons

Northern Harrier
Broad-Winged Hawk
Cooper's Hawk
Red-Shouldered Hawk
Red-Tailed Hawk

Sharp-Shinned Hawk
American Kestrel
Merlin
Osprey
Turkey Vulture

Warblers, Blackbirds, and Tanagers

Brown-Headed Catbird
Yellow-Breasted Chat
Boat-Tailed Grackle
Orchard Oriole
Northern Oriole
Ovenbird
Northern Parula
American Redstart
House Sparrow
European Starling
Scarlet Tanager
Bay-Breasted Warbler
Black-Throated Blue Warbler
Black-Throated Green Warbler
Black-and-White Warbler
Blackburnian Warbler

Blue-Winged Warbler
Canada Warbler
Cape May Warbler
Chestnut-Sided Warbler
Magnolia Warbler
Mourning Warbler
Nashville Warbler
Palm Warbler
Prairie Warbler
Tennessee Warbler
Wilson's Warbler
Yellow Warbler
Yellow-Rumped Warbler
Northern Waterthrush
Common Yellowthroat

Summer

Ducks

American Black Duck
Wood Duck

Mallards
Blue-Winged Teal

Finches and Sparrows

Northern Cardinal
House Finch
American Goldfinch

Field Sparrow
Swamp Sparrow

Flycatchers, Swallows, Jays, and Crows

Fish Crow
Eastern Kingbird

Barn Swallow

Herons, Egrets, and Ibises

Great Egret
Snowy Egret
Great Blue Heron

Green Heron
Little Blue Heron

Kingfishers

Belted Kingfisher

Kinglets and Vireos

Red-Eyed Vireo
White-Eyed Vireo

Cedar Waxwing

Pigeons to Woodpeckers

Mourning Dove
Rock Dove

Ruby-Throated Hummingbird

Plovers, Sandpipers, Gulls, and Terns

Short-Billed Dowitcher
Great Black-Backed Gull

Laughing Gull
Ring-Billed Gull

Killdeer
Black-Bellied Plover
Piping Plover
Sanderling
Least Sandpiper
Semipalmated Sandpiper
Solitary Sandpiper
Spotted Sandpiper

Western Sandpiper
Black Skimmer
Common Tern
Least Tern
Willet
American Woodcock
Greater Yellowlegs
Lesser Yellowlegs

Rails

Clapper Rail

Virginia Rail

Titmice, Wrens, and Mimic Thrushes

Black-Capped Chickadee
Northern Mockingbird

American Robin
House Wren

Vultures, Hawks, Ospreys, and Falcons

Red-Tailed Hawk
Osprey

Turkey Vulture

Warblers and Blackbirds

Blackpoll
Yellow-Breasted Chat
Brown-Headed Cowbird
Common Grackle

American Redstart
Prairie Warbler
Yellow Warbler

Autumn

Flycatchers, Swallows, Jays, and Crows

Fish Crow
Great-Crested Flycatcher
Least Flycatcher

Yellow-Bellied Flycatcher
Blue Jay
Eastern Kingbird

Horned Lark
Eastern Wood Pewee
Eastern Phoebe

Bank Swallow
Barn Swallow
Tree Swallow

Grebes and Cormorants

Double-Crested Cormorant
Great Cormorant

Northern Gannet
Horned Grebe

Grosbeaks, Finches, and Sparrows

Indigo Bunting
Snow Bunting
Northern Cardinal
House Finch
Purple Finch
American Goldfinch
Evening Grosbeak
Rose-Breasted Grosbeak
Pine Siskin

American Tree Sparrow
Chipping Sparrow
Field Sparrow
Fox Sparrow
House Sparrow
Savannah Sparrow
Swamp Sparrow
Vesper Sparrow
White-Crowned Sparrow

Herons, Egrets, and Bitterns

American Bittern
Great Egret
Snowy Egret

Great Blue Heron
Green Heron
Little Blue Heron

Kinglets, Shrikes, and Vireos

Eastern Bluebird
Golden-Crowned Kinglet
Ruby-Crowned Kinglet
Red-Eyed Vireo

Solitary Vireo
White-Eyed Vireo
Cedar Waxwing

Kingfishers

Belted Kingfisher

Loons

Common Loon

Red-Throated Loon

Pigeons to Woodpeckers

Mourning Dove
Rock Dove

Ruby-Throated Hummingbird

Plovers, Sandpipers, Gulls, and Terns

Long-Billed Dowitcher
Dunlin
Bonaparte's Gull
Great Black-Backed Gull
Laughing Gull
Ring-Billed Gull
Killdeer
American Golden Plover
Black-Bellied Plover
Piping Plover
Semipalmated Plover
Sanderling
Least Sandpiper

Pectoral Sandpiper
Semipalmated Sandpiper
Spotted Sandpiper
Western Sandpiper
White-Rumped Sandpiper
Common Snipe
Least Tern
Royal Tern
Ruddy Turnstone
Willet
American Woodcock
Greater Yellowlegs
Lesser Yellowlegs

Rails and Coots

American Coot

Clapper Rail

Swans, Geese, and Ducks

Bufflehead
Canvasback
American Black Duck
Ruddy Duck
Wood Duck
Common Goldeneye
Canada Goose

Snow Goose
Mallard
Red-Breasted Merganser
Oldsquaw
Lesser Scaup
Surf Scoter Black Scoter
White-Winged Scoter

Mute Swan

Blue-Winged Teal

Green-Winged Teal

American Wigeon

Titmice, Nuthatches, Wrens, and Mimic Thrushes

Gray Catbird

Black-Capped Chickadee

Brown Creeper

Northern Mockingbird

Red-Breasted Nuthatch

American Robin

Brown Thrasher

Gray-Cheeked Thrush

Hermit Thrush

Swainson's Thrush

House Wren

Winter Wren

Vultures, Hawks, Osprey, and Falcons

Northern Harrier

Broad-Winged Hawk

Cooper's Hawk

Red-Shouldered Hawk

Red-Tailed Hawk

Rough-Legged Hawk

Sharp-Shinned Hawk

American Kestrel

Merlin

Osprey

Turkey Vulture

Warblers, Blackbirds, and Tanagers

Blackpoll

Bobolink

Yellow-Breasted Chat

Brown-Headed Cowbird

Common Grackle

Northern Oriole

Ovenbird

Northern Parula

American Redstart

Scarlet Tanager

Bay-Breasted Warbler

Black-and-White Warbler

Black-Throated Blue Warbler

Black-Throated Green Warbler

Blackburnian Warbler

Canada Warbler

Cape May Warbler

Chestnut-Sided Warbler

Magnolia Warbler

Mourning Warbler

Nashville Warbler

Orange-Crowned Warbler

Palm Warbler

Tennessee Warbler

Yellow Warbler

Northern Waterthrush

Common Yellowthroat

Flycatchers, Swallows, Jays, and Crows

Horned Lark

Grebes

Horned Grebe

Grosbeaks, Finches, and Sparrows

Snow Bunting
Northern Cardinal
House Finch
American Goldfinch
Evening Grosbeak
Dark-Eyed Junco
Pine Siskin

American Tree Sparrow
Field Sparrow
Fox Sparrow
Savannah Sparrow
Swamp Sparrow
White-Throated Sparrow

Herons

Great Blue Heron

Kinglets

Golden-Crowned Kinglet

Loons

Common Loon

Red-Throated Loon

Owls

Great Horned Owl

Pigeons and Doves

Mourning Dove

Rock Dove

Plovers, Sandpipers, Gulls, and Terns

Dunlin
Bonaparte's Gull
Ring-Billed Gull

Black-Bellied Plover
Sanderling
Ruddy Turnstone

Swans, Geese, and Ducks

Brant
Bufflehead
Canvasback
Ruddy Duck
Common Goldeneye
Canada Goose
Mallard
Common Merganser

Red-Breasted Merganser
Redhead
Lesser Scaup
Black Scoter
Surf Scoter
White-Winged Scoter
Green-Winged Teal

Titmice, Nuthatches, Wrens, and Mimic Thrushes

Black-Capped Chickadee
Brown Creeper
Northern Mockingbird

Red-Breasted Nuthatch
American Robin
Tufted Titmouse

Vultures, Hawks, Osprey, and Falcons

Northern Harrier
Red-Tailed Hawk
Rough-Legged Hawk

Sharp-Shinned Hawk
American Kestrel
Merlin

Warblers and Blackbirds

Red-Winged Blackbird
Brown-Headed Cowbird

House Sparrow
Yellow-Rumped Warbler

Woodpeckers

Northern Flicker
Yellow-Bellied Sapsucker

Downy Woodpecker

Plainsboro Preserve: The New Kid on the Audubon Block

HISTORY

The Plainsboro Preserve is New Jersey Audubon Society's newest property. Originally acquired by the Township of Plainsboro for $2.9 million in open space funds, the Society partnered with the township in 2000 to turn the preserve into a viable nature and education center.

TERRAIN

The property's 630 acres of open space, in the flat meadows of Central Jersey's Piedmont area, sit between the historic town of Princeton and Route 1. The area is one of the state's busiest and most congested corridors that best demonstrates urban sprawl.

Plainsboro Preserve
Scotts Corner Road
P.O. Box 446
Plainsboro, NJ 08536
Phone: (609) 897-9400

Hours: Tuesday through
Sunday, 9 A.M. to 5 P.M.
Closed Mondays and
holidays. Trails open
daily dawn to dusk.

Facilities:
Environmental
Education Center under
construction. When
completed, it will
include a nature center,
resource library, book
and gift store,
interpretive displays,
model gardens, and an
observation deck.

McCormack Lake

All noise and turmoil, however, are
forgotten as soon as you enter the
preserve's driveway, park in the gravel
lot, and start walking. Situated in the
central part of New Jersey, Plainsboro
is an excellent example of the
Piedmont part of the state: part wetlands, part floodplains, part woods,
meadows, and fields.

Tree Swallows

TRAILS

Five miles of trails take
you through beech woods
and meadows lined with
brush that is thick with warblers in spring. Bluebirds
flock to the houses waiting
for them alongside 50-acre
McCormack Lake. It's

How to Get Here

From the North: The direct way is to take Route 287 South to the exit for the New Jersey Turnpike. Take the Turnpike south and proceed to U.S. Route 1. From Route 1, proceed to the Scudders Mills Road exit. At the fifth traffic light (Dey Road), turn left. Proceed east to the first traffic light, which is Scotts Corner Road. Turn left. The preserve is about one-quarter of a mile beyond the community park on your left.

From the South: Follow the Garden State Parkway to the turnpike entrance and proceed south on the turnpike to exit ?. Follow directions from Route 1, above.

Note: With its seemingly pervasive road construction, traffic clots and strip malls, Route 1 can become a nightmare. The more scenic route from the north is to take Route 287 to the Somerville exit. Follow the signs for 202/206 South and then pick up Route 206 south to Princeton. Go as far as you can in Princeton until you come to a T-intersection. Do not follow Route 206 to the right! Rather, bear left, take the next right (this is actually a large curve), and turn left onto Alexander Road. Follow Alexander Road all the way to Route 1 and turn left onto that highway. Proceed north to Scudders Mill Road. Follow directions above.

common to hear the shrill calls of an osprey before you see it fly overhead, searching the waters for a fishy treat.

According to New Jersey Audubon, more than 150 species of birds call the preserve home. Like Scherman-Hoffman

Eastern Bluebird

Wildlife Sanctuary, species include worm-eating and cerulean warblers, Eastern bluebirds, pileated woodpeckers, black-capped chickadees, yellow-shafted flickers, red-bellied woodpeckers, wild turkeys, and great-horned and Eastern screech owls. Rarities occur.

There are least 10 species of endangered wildflowers, including the southern twayblade orchid. As you'll see, Plainsboro also has the most extensive plant list of all the centers.

BIRDS

Note: Plainsboro Preserve is so new that seasonal migration patterns have not been documented. Because of this, the following bird list cannot be broken into seasonal lists. Contact the preserve for more information.

Bitterns, Grebes, and Loons

American Bittern
Double-Crested Cormorant

Pied-Billed Grebe
Common Loon

Blackbirds to Tanagers

Bobolink
Red-Winged Blackbird
Yellow-Breasted Chat
Brown-Headed Cowbird

Common Grackle
Eastern Meadowlark
Baltimore Oriole

Flycatchers to Vireos

Alder Flycatcher
Great-Crested Flycatcher
Willow Flycatcher
Eastern Kingbird

Eastern Wood Pewee
Eastern Phoebe
Red-Eyed Vireo
Warbling Vireo

Grosbeaks, Finches, and Sparrows

Indigo Bunting
Snow Bunting
Northern Cardinal
House Finch
American Goldfinch
Blue Grosbeak
Rose-Breasted Grosbeak
Dark-Eyed Junco
Common Redpoll
American Tree Sparrow

Chipping Sparrow
Field Sparrow
House Sparrow
Savannah Sparrow
Song Sparrow
Swamp Sparrow
White-Throated Sparrow
Scarlet Tanager
Eastern Towhee

Grouse, Quails, and Turkeys

Northern Bobwhite
Roughed Grouse

Ring-Necked Pheasant

Herons, Egrets, and Ibises

Cattle Egret
Great Egret
Snowy Egret
Great Blue Heron

Green Heron
Little Blue Heron
Glossy Ibis

Jays to Wrens

Black-Capped Chickadee
Carolina Chickadee
Brown Creeper
American Crow
Fish Crow
Blue Jay
Purple Martin
Red-Breasted Nuthatch
White-Breasted Nuthatch

Bank Swallow
Barn Swallow
Cliff Swallow
Northern Rough-Winged Swallow
Tree Swallow
Tufted Titmouse
Carolina Wren
House Wren
Winter Wren

Kinglets to Waxwings

Eastern Bluebird
Gray Catbird
Blue-Gray Gnatcatcher
Golden-Crowned Kinglet
Ruby-Crowned Kinglet
Northern Mockingbird
American Robin

European Starling
Brown Thrasher
Hermit Thrush
Swainson's Thrush
Wood Thrush
Veery
Cedar Waxwing

Plovers, Sandpipers, Gulls, and Terns

Killdeer
Great Black-Backed Gull
Herring Gull
Laughing Gull
Ring-Billed Gull

Solitary Sandpiper
Spotted Sandpiper
Upland Sandpiper
Common Snipe
American Woodcock

Pigeons to Woodpeckers

Black-Billed Cuckoo
Yellow-Billed Cuckoo
Mourning Dove
Rock Dove
Northern Flicker
Ruby-Throated Hummingbird
Belted Kingfisher

Common Nighthawk
Yellow-Bellied Sapsucker
Chimney Swift
Downy Woodpecker
Hairy Woodpecker
Red-Bellied Woodpecker

Rails and Coots

American Coot
King Rail

Virginia Rail

Raptors and Vultures

Bald Eagle
Peregrine Falcon

Northern Harrier
Broad-Winged Hawk

Cooper's Hawk
Red-Tailed Hawk
American Kestrel
Osprey
Barred Owl

Eastern Screech Owl
Great Horned Owl
Northern Saw-Whet Owl
Black Vulture
Turkey Vulture

Swans, Geese, and Ducks

Bufflehead
American Black Duck
Ring-Necked Duck
Ruddy Duck
Wood Duck
Gadwall
Canada Goose
Snow Goose
Mallard

Common Merganser
Red-Breasted Merganser
Greater Scaup
Lesser Scaup
Surf Scoter
Mute Swan
Tundra Swan
Green-Winged Teal

Warblers

Blackpoll
Ovenbird
Northern Parula
American Redstart
Black-and-White Warbler
Black-Throated Blue Warbler
Blue-Winged Warbler
Canada Warbler
Cape May Warbler
Chestnut-Sided Warbler

Magnolia Warbler
Nashville Warbler
Pine Warbler
Prairie Warbler
Tennessee Warbler
Yellow Warbler
Yellow-Rumped Warbler
Northern Waterthrush
Common Yellowthroat

PLANTS

Note: Ferns and plants are presented in alphabetical order by species in English rather than broken down by Latin species to make it easier for first-time visitors.

Ferns and Fern Allies

Bracken
Appressed Bog Clubmoss
Staghorn Clubmoss
Tree Clubmoss
Boott's Fern
Christmas Fern
Cinnamon Fern
Cut-Leaved Grape Fern
Interrupted Fern
Lady Fern
Marsh Fern
Netted Chain Fern

Royal Fern
Sensitive Fern
Virginia Fern
Field Horsetail
Common Running Pine
Shortleaf Pine
Virginia Pine
White Pine
Common Polypody
Quillwort
Ebony Spleenwort
Norway Spruce

Flowering plants

Tall Hairy Agrimony
Smoothe Alder
Alfalfa
Wood Anemone
Apple
Broadleaved Arrowhead
Arrowwood
Arrow Arum
Green or Red Ash
White Ash
Asparagus
Bigtooth Aspen
Quaking Aspen
Bushy Aster
Calico Aster
Heath Aster
New England Aster
New York Aster
Panicled Aster
Small White Aster
White Wood Aster
Swamp Azalea
Japanese Barberry

Basswood
Bayberry
Small-Headed Beaked-Rush
Trailing Wild Bean
Showy Goat's Beard
Beech
Beechdrops
Sessile Bellwort
Creeping Bent
Bouncing Bet
Field Bindweed
Black Birch
Gray Birch
River Birch
Hairy Bittercress
Pennsylvania Bittercress
Mountain Blackberry
Highbush Blueberry
Late Lowbush Blueberry
Annual Bluegrass
Canada Bluegrass
Kentucky Bluegrass
Rough Bluegrass

Woodland Bluegrass
Little Bluestem
Boneset
Climbing Boneset
Upland Boneset
Virgin's Bower
Hairy Brome
Japanese Brome
Climbing False Buckwheat
Upright Bugleweed
Softstem Bullrush
Branching Bur-Reed
Common Burdock
Butter and Eggs
Bulbous Buttercup
Kidney-Leaved Buttercup
Tall Buttercup
Buttonbush
Buttonweed
Skunk Cabbage
White Campion
Catnip
Northern Catulpa
Wild Celery
Field Chamomile
Choke Cherry
Wild Black Cherry
Chess
Downy Chess
Hairy Chess
American Chestnut
Common Chickweed
Mouse-Ear Chickweed
Chicory
Common Cinquefoil
Dwarf Cinquefoil
Rough Cinquefoil
Clayton's Bedstraw
Clearweed
Cleavers

Common Clotbur
Hairy Bush Clover
Rabbit Foot Clover
Red Clover
Round-Headed Bush Clover
Silky Bush Clover
Slender Bush Clover
Wand-Like Bush Clover
White Clover
White Sweet Clover
Yellow Hop-Clover
Yellow Sweet Clover
Corn
Cottonwood
Cowbane
Sweet Crabapple
Carolina Cranesbill
Virginia Creeper
Common Winter Cress
Mouse-Ear Cress
Indian Cucumber-Root
Blue Curls
Two-Flowered Cynthia
Daffodil
Oxeye Daisy
Dandelion
Dwarf Dandelion
Asiatic Dayflower
Tawny Daylily
Deerberry
Northern Dewberry
Swamp Dewberry
Curled Dock
Common Dodder
Dogbane
Clasping-Leaved Dogbane
Flowering Dogwood
Red Osier Dogwood
Silky Dogwood
Lesser Duckweed

Large Mouse Ear
Common Elder
Pearly Everlasting
Sweet Fern
Meadow Fescue
Red Fescue
Six-Weeks Fescue
Tall Fescue
Fetterbush
Larger Blue Flag
Slender Blue Flag
Stiff Yellow Flax
Daisy Fleabane
Philadelphia Fleabane
Cardinal Flower
Pinxter Flower
Small Forget-Me-Not
Foxtail
Marsh Foxtail
Meadow Foxtail
Field Garlic
Wild Geranium
Purple Gerardia
Gill-Over-The-Ground
Dwarf Ginseng
Ivy-Leaved Morning Glory
Blue-Stemmed Goldenrod
Canada Goldenrod
Downy Goldenrod
Early Goldenrod
Elm-Leaved Goldenrod
Grass-Leaved Goldenrod
Gray Goldenrod
Rough-Stemmed Goldenrod
Smooth Goldenrod
Sweet Goldenrod
Zig-Zag Goldenrod
Fox Grape
Summer Grape
Barnyard Grass

Blue-Eyed Grass
Deertongue Grass
Orange Grass
Orchard Grass
Panic Grass
Poverty Grass
Quack Grass
Reed Canary Grass
Stilt Grass
Sweet Vernal Grass
Switch Grass
Whitelow Grass
Wool Grass
Common Greenbrier
Glaucous Greenbrier
Groundnut
Groundsel
Sour Gum
Sweet Gum
Field Hawkweed
Pale Hawkweed
Hawthorn
Heal All
Henbit
Shagbark Hickory
American Holly
Japanese Honeysuckle
Tartarian Honeysuckle
Cut-Leaved Water Horehound
Purple Water Horehound
Hop Hornbeam
Wild Indigo
New York Ironweed
Poison Ivy
Downy Juneberry
Spotted Knapweed
Japanese Knotweed
Queen Anne's Lace
Lady's Thumb
Pink Lady-Slipper

Mountain Laurel
Lily-of-the-Valley
Trout Lily
Turk's-Cap Lily
Black Locust
Venus's Looking Glass
Purple Loosestrife
Swamp Loosestrife
Whorled Loosestrife
Magnolia
Sweet Bay Magnolia
Floating Manna-Grass
Fowl Manna-Grass
Red Maple
Silver Maple
Mayapple
Meadowsweet
Periwinkle
Virginia Meadow Beauty
MilkweedSwamp Milkweed
Purple Milkwort
Narrow-Leaved Mountain Mint
Mugwort
Red Mulberry
White Mulberry
Common Mullein
Moth Mullein
Field Mustard
Garlic Mustard
Horse Nettle
Purple Dead Nettle
Bittersweet Nightshade
Yellow Nutsedge
Nodding Ladies Tresses
Pin Oak
Red Oak
Swamp White Oak
White Oak
Willow Oak
Autumn Olive

Mock Orange
Wild Pansy
Partridgeberry
Everlasting Pea
Mild Water Pepper
Sweet Pepperbush
Prairie Peppergrass
Pilewort
Short-Stalked False Pimpernel
Deptford Pink
Indian Pipe
Wild Sensitive Plant
American Plantain
Bracted Plantain
Common Plantain
English Plantain
Small Water Plantain
Pokeweed
Pondweed
Small-Leaved Pondweed
Tape-Leaved Pondweed
Thin-Leaved Pondweed
Balsam Poplar
Plume Poppy
Evening Primrose
Jack-In-The-Pulpit
Purpletop
Water Purslane
Lamb's Quarters
Common Ragweed
Golden Ragwort
Black Raspberry
Rattlebox
Common Reed
Dame's Rocket
Multiflora Rose
Swamp Rose
Tall Meadow Rue
Canada Rush
Path Rush

Sharp-Fruited Rush
Soft Rush
Twig Rush
Rye
Perennial Ryegrass
Canada St. Johnswort
Common St. Johnswort
Dwarf St. Johnswort
Marsh St. Johnswort
Spotted St. Johnswort
Sassafras
Atlantic Sedge
Awl-Fruited Sedge
Bladder Sedge
Broom Sedge
Fox Sedge
Fringed Sedge
Gray's Sedge
Hairy-Fruited Sedge
Hop Sedge
Lake-Bank Sedge
Long Sedge
Nodding Sedge
Pointed Broom Sedge
Sallow Sedge
Slender Sedge
Swan's Sedge
Thicket Sedge
Three-Way Sedge
Tussock Sedge
White-Edged Sedge
Yellow-Fruited Sedge
Seedbox
Shadbush
Silverrod
Hyssop Skullcap
Mad-Dog Skullcap
White Snakeroot
Solomon's Seal
False Solomon's Seal

Pennsylvania Smartweed
Common Wood Sorrel
Sheep Sorrel
Southern Yellow Wood Sorrel
Soybean
Spatterdock
Common Speedwell
Corn Speedwell
Ivy-Leafed Speedwell
Persian Speedwell
Purslane Speedwell
Thyme-Leaved Speedwell
Spicebush
Blunt Spike-Rush
Slender Spike-Rush
Spring Beauty
Square-Stemed Monkey Flower
Foxglove Beadtongue
Star of Bethlehem
Star Flower
Steeplebush
Lesser Stitchwort
Ditch Stonecrop
Indian Strawberry
Wild Strawberry
Swamp Candles
Dwarf Sumac
Smooth Sumac
Staghorn Sumac
Small Sundrops
Southern Sundrops
Northern Tickseed Sunflower
Showy Sunflower
Tall Sunflower
Sycamore
Arrow-Leaved Tearthumb
Halberd-Leaved Tearthumb
Bull Thistle
Canada Thistle
Hyssop-Leaved Thoroughwort

Late-Flowering Thoroughwort
White Thoroughwort
Tick-Trefoil
Panicled Tick-Trefoil
Showy Tick-Trefoil
Smooth Small-Leaved Tick-Trefoil
Ticklegrass
Purple-Stemmed Beggar Ticks
Small Beggar Ticks
Timothy
Bastard Toadflax
Blue Toadflax
Indian Tobacco
Spotted Touch-Me-Not
Tree of Heaven
Empress Tree
Turtlehead
Southern Twayblade
Blue Vernain
Barrow-Leaved Vetch
Slender Vetch
Linden Viburnum
Maple-Leaved Viburnum
Arrow-Leaved Violet
Dooryard Violet
Lance-Leaved Violet

Marsh Blue Violet
Northern White Violet
Primrose-Leaved Violet
Sweet White Violet
Black Walnut
Waterweed
Eastern Joe Pye Weed
Mermaid Weed
Pickerel Weed
Pineapple Weed
Sweet-Scented Joe Pye Weed
Wheat
Slender Wheatgrass
Wild Four O'Clock
Black Willow
Dwarf Willow
Pussy Willow
Purple-Leaved Willow-Herb
Winterberry
. Smooth Winterberry
Spotted Wintergreen
Pointed Wolffia
Common Woodrush
Spiny Woodrush
Yarrow

Chapter Six

Rancocas Nature Center: The One-Dollar Haven

HISTORY

With its 130-year-old farmhouse and intriguing trail loop, the Rancocas Nature Center has been part of the New Jersey Audubon Society since 1977.

Not a bad deal, for a buck. It was that year that Society board member Elmer Rowley set out to find a location for an education facility similar to that of the Lorrimer and Scherman-Hoffman centers.

Rowley found a location in the shape of an old farmhouse in Burlington County near Rancocas State Park. The Society could lease it from the state for the grand price of $1 a year for five years. The Society renovated the old house, built in 1869, and the center was officially opened in October of 1977.

**Rancocas Nature
Center**
794 Rancocas Road
Mount Holly, NJ
08060
Phone: (609) 261-2495
E-mail: rancocas@
njaudubon.org

Hours: Tuesday
through Saturday, 9
A.M. to 5 P.M.; Sunday,
11 A.M. to 5 P.M.
Closed Mondays and
Holidays. Trails open
daily to 5 P.M.

Facilities: Museum,
book and gift shop,
library, classroom
available for group
meetings, lectures,
presentations. The
center also offers a
wide variety of
eco-travel programs.

The Farmhouse

TERRAIN

Easy to access from the frenetic
New Jersey Turnpike, the center is a
120-acre refuge of calm set amid the
distinct and diverse characteristics of
southwestern New Jersey: part clay marsh, part uplands woods,
part fields. The habitats are the perfect draw for a variety of bird
life, making it the naturalist's ideal classroom.

The Nature Center is a pleasant stop for getting out and
stretching your legs. If you take its trail loop at a brisk pace,
you'll move through in about 15 to 20 minutes. Meander, and

How to Get Here

From North and South: From the Garden State Parkway and/or Route 287, follow signs to the New Jersey Turnpike South to Exit 5 (Burlington/Mount Holly). Follow the ramp and turn onto Burlington/Mount Holly Road. Stay on Burlington/Mount Holly Road for about a mile and bear right onto Mount Holly Bypass.

The road sign is small and difficult to see. A Burger King sits to the right of the highway, at the turn: Look for it and turn there. From here, turn right onto Rancocas Road and follow it for about a mile. The sign for the center will be on your left.

From Interstate 295, take Exit 45A (Mount Holly-Willingboro) and proceed east on Rancocas Road for about two miles. The center will be on your right-hand side.

If you live locally, take Route 206 to Route 38 and go west to the Route 541 bypass. Turn right and continue on to Rancocas Road. The center will be on your left.

you'll enjoy a walk that holds a wide variety of natural wonders.

TRAILS

Rancocas's trail loop is short—less than one mile. It is relatively flat and can be covered in a reasonably short time,

Entrance

The Old Shed

providing you don't stop to investigate its plentiful assortment of bird and plant life. Jammed into the short loop, which covers a variety of woods and fields that run along Rancocas Creek, are more than 200 types of plants and 100 species of birds.

The trail starts at the end of the driveway, near the center's old, whitewashed barn and an equipment shed, whose rusted condition is a sign that it has seen better days. The trail loops to the right. Along the way you'll pass a field where you may be lucky to glimpse northern harriers and kestrels hunting for the random vole or sparrow. Ring-necked pheasants, bobwhite, and goldfinches can also be sighted. As you continue on, you enter a conifer grove that includes white pines, scaly barked Austrian pines, spruce trees, and larches. The grove is nearly barren of wildlife, but its serenity and heady conifer scent are worth the pause.

The trail bears to the right. You'll enter an area filled with American holly and oak trees, followed by an area of sweet gum, whose fruit, which resembles a golf-ball–sized mace, is a favorite among the local squirrels. The trash dump you encounter is a reminder to visitors to care for the environment.

Markers along the trail point to subjects of interest, and change from season to season. If you're curious, pick up the trail flier at the center.

SIDE TRIPS

As long as you're in the southwest portion of New Jersey and you want to explore other areas, you may want to backtrack to Route 295 and continue south to Exit 10. Bear right, and follow Center Square Road through an industrial park. Go straight through the light and turn left at a four-way intersection with a small white island in the center: This is Predricktown Road. Continue straight on the road until just before a small causeway and park on the grassy shoulder. You'll find yourself at Oldman's Creek and the Pedricktown Causeway. Like most of the marshes, ponds, and creeks that thread through Salem and Gloucester counties, the spot is excellent for eyeing pied-billed grebes, northern pintails, mergansers, bald eagles, green-winged teal and the occasional Eurasian wigeon.

Some of the state's best grassland birding is in this part of the state. From Route 40, pick up Route 45 West at Woodstown to the King's Highway and continue to Sharptown-Audubon Road north. The first crossroads is Feather-bed Lane. Both of these roads are prime wintering grounds for thousands of snow geese,

Forest

with the occasional, smaller Ross's goose thrown in for good measure.

It's fun to park along the road and look for that random "blue" goose, the immature snow goose whose down looks almost like a dark slate blue.

Driving around the narrow country roads, with their acres and acres of flat farmlands, is a bit like driving back in time. Small wonder: Pennsville Township was originally founded in the mid-17th century by Swedish, Finnish, and later Dutch, immigrants.

The area also has a distinct feel of the South. Predricktown has the cozy laziness of Fredricksburg, Virginia, while smaller bergs like Auburn contain two-story brick houses with decorative latticework reminiscent of the antebellum architecture of the Old South.

One other note: I was so intent on birding it took me some time to realize why orange and black signs bearing emergency information were prominently positioned on all the roads. This part of southern New Jersey sits in the shadow of a nuclear power plant.

Continuing on Route 49 South will eventually take you to the foot of the Delaware Memorial Bridge and Fort Mott State Park, which was built at the end of the 19th century to defend the entrance to Philadelphia. Peapatch Island, the largest heron rookery north of Florida, can be seen from here.

Supawna Meadows National Wildlife Refuge, one of New Jersey's five National Wildlife Refuges, is east of the fort but is not open to the public.

After your jaunt around Salem and Gloucester counties you can backtrack north on Route 295 to Exit 10 to visit New Jersey Audubon's Twin Islands Preserve (see p. 165).

BIRDS

Coots

American Coot

Cuckoos

Black-Billed Cuckoo　　　　　　Yellow-Billed Cuckoo

Flycatchers, Swallows, Jays, and Crows

American Crow　　　　　　Eastern Wood Pewee
Fish Crow　　　　　　Eastern Phoebe
Great-Crested Flycatcher　　　　　　Bank Swallow
Blue Jay　　　　　　Barn Swallow
Eastern Kingbird　　　　　　Rough-Winged Swallow
Purple Martin　　　　　　Tree Swallow

Geese and Ducks

Canada Goose　　　　　　Mallard
American Black Duck　　　　　　Hooded Merganser
Ring-Necked Duck　　　　　　Northern Pintail
Wood Duck　　　　　　Blue-Winged Teal

Grebes

Double-Crested Cormorant　　　　　　Pied-Billed Grebe

Grosbeaks, Finches, and Sparrows

Red-Winged Blackbird
Rusty Blackbird
Bobolink
Indigo Bunting
Northern Cardinal
Brown-Headed Cowbird
White-Winged Crossbill
House Finch
Purple Finch
American Goldfinch
Common Grackle
Rose-Breasted Grosbeak
Dark-Eyed Junco
Eastern Meadowlark

Northern Oriole
Orchard Oriole
Common Redpoll
Pine Siskin
American Tree Sparrow
Chipping Sparrow
Field Sparrow
Fox Sparrow
House Sparrow
Song Sparrow
Swamp Sparrow
White-Crowned Sparrow
White-Throated Sparrow
Rufous-Sided Towhee

Herons

Great Blue Heron

Green Heron

Kingfishers

Belted Kingfisher

Kinglets and Vireos

Eastern Bluebird
Blue-Gray Gnatcatcher
Golden-Crowned Kinglet
Ruby-Crowned Kinglet
European Starling
Philadelphia Vireo

Red-Eyed Vireo
Solitary Vireo
White-Eyed Vireo
Yellow-Throated Vireo
Cedar Waxwing

Owls

Barred Owl
Eastern Screech Owl

Great Horned Owl
Long-Eared Owl

Sunset, Sunset Beach, Cape May

Dunes, Cape May Point

Cranberry Viburnum, Goshen

Early Morning Walk

Great Egret, Sandy Hook

Wood Ducks

Thistle, Scherman-Hoffman

Sandy Hook Towhee

Eastern Swallowtail, Scherman-Hoffman

Sunset in "The Meadows," Northwood Center

Lorrimer Wildflower

Pond Lilies at Goshen

Autumn at Scherman-Hoffman

Goldenrod in "The Meadows," Northwood Center

Cape May Point State Park

Cape May Point Hawk Watch

Autumn Migration Statistics

	This Year			History	
SPECIES	YESTERDAY'S TOTAL	TOTAL TO DATE	PEAK FLIGHT AND DATE	RECORD DAILY TOTAL AND DATE	RECORD ANNUAL TOTAL AND YEAR
Black Vulture		116		32 OCT 31 98	370 97
Turkey Vulture		776		784 NOV 3 96	6420 96
Osprey		1904		1023 OCT 3 89	6734 96
Bald Eagle		131		24 SEP 19 96	284 96
Northern Harrier		743		278 NOV 12 80	3115 94
Sharp-Shinned Hawk		15663		11096 OCT 4 77	61167 84
Cooper's Hawk		2613		456 OCT 3 94	5009 95
Northern Goshawk		12		13	89 97
Red-Shouldered Hawk		232		165 NOV 10 94	872 94
Broad-Winged Hawk		1905		9400 OCT 4 77	13918 81
Swainson's Hawk		0		3	10 98
Red-Tailed Hawk		1162		1022 NOV 11 94	5135 96
Rough-Legged Hawk		1		4 NOV 13 83	13 99
Golden Eagle		10		8 NOV 3 96	38 96
American Kestrel		6393		5038 SEP 30 99	21821 81
Merlin		1086		867 SEP 30 99	2875 85
Peregrine Falcon		988		291 OCT 7 97	1793 97
TOTAL					

Counting Hawks at Cape May Point

Sunset Birding, "The Meadows," Northwood Center

Birders, Cape May Point

Great Egret

Birder's Break, Higbee Beach, Northwood Center

Cabbage White, Scherman-Hoffman

Winter, Scherman-Hoffman Wildlife Sanctuary

Pigeons and Doves

Mourning Dove

Rock Dove

Plovers, Sandpipers, and Gulls

Herring Gull
Laughing Gull
Ring-Billed Gull
Killdeer
Least Sandpiper
Solitary Sandpiper

Spotted Sandpiper
Common Snipe
American Woodcock
Greater Yellowlegs
Lesser Yellowlegs

Quails

Northern Bobwhite

Ringed-Necked Pheasant

Swifts and Hummingbirds

Ruby-Throated Hummingbird

Chimney Swift

Titmice, Nuthatches, Wrens, and Mimic Thrushes

Gray Catbird
Black-Capped Chickadee
Carolina Chickadee
Brown Creeper
Northern Mockingbird
Red-Breasted Nuthatch
White-Breasted Nuthatch
American Robin

Brown Thrasher
Hermit Thrush
Swainson's Thrush
Wood Thrush
Tufted Titmouse
Veery
Carolina Wren
House Wren

Vultures, Hawks, Osprey, and Falcons

Northern Harrier
Broad-Winged Hawk
Cooper's Hawk

Red-Shouldered Hawk
Red-Tailed Hawk
Sharp-Shinned Hawk

American Kestrel
Osprey

Turkey Vulture

Warblers, Blackbirds, and Tanagers

Blackpoll
Yellow-Breasted Chat
Ovenbird
Northern Parula
American Redstart
Scarlet Tanager
Bay-Breasted Warbler
Black-Throated Blue Warbler
Black-Throated Green Warbler
Black-and-White Warbler
Blackburnian Warbler
Blue-Winged Warbler
Canada Warbler

Cape May Warbler
Chestnut-Sided Warbler
Hooded Warbler
Magnolia Warbler
Mourning Warbler
Nashville Warbler
Palm Warbler
Pine Warbler
Tennessee Warbler
Yellow Warbler
Northern Waterthrush
Common Yellowthroat

Woodpeckers

Northern Flicker
Yellow-Bellied Sapsucker
Downy Woodpecker

Hairy Woodpecker
Pileated Woodpecker
Red-Bellied Woodpecker

Summer

Cuckoos

Yellow-Billed Cuckoo

Flycatchers, Swallows, Jays, and Crows

American Crow
Fish Crow

Great-Crested Flycatcher
Blue Jay

Eastern Kingbird
Purple Martin
Eastern Wood Pewee
Eastern Phoebe

Bank Swallow
Barn Swallow
Rough-Winged Swallow
Tree Swallow

Geese and Ducks

American Black Duck
Canada Goose

Mallard

Grosbeaks, Finches, and Sparrows

Red-Winged Blackbird
Bobolink
Indigo Bunting
Northern Cardinal
Brown-Headed Cowbird
House Finch
American Goldfinch
Common Grackle

Blue Grosbeak
Eastern Meadowlark
Northern Oriole
Chipping Sparrow
Field Sparrow
Song Sparrow
Swamp Sparrow
Rufous-Sided Towhee

Herons

Great Blue Heron

Green Heron

Kingfishers

Belted Kingfisher

Kinglets and Vireos

Blue-Gray Gnatcatcher
European Starling
Red-Eyed Vireo

White-Eyed Vireo
Cedar Waxwing

Owls

Barred Owl
Eastern Screech Owl

Great Horned Owl

Pigeons and Doves

Mourning Dove

Rock Dove

Plovers, Sandpipers, and Gulls

Laughing Gull
Killdeer

American Woodcock

Quails

Northern Bobwhite

Ringed-Necked Pheasant

Swifts and Hummingbirds

Ruby-Throated Hummingbird

Chimney Swift

Titmice, Nuthatches, Wrens, and Mimic Thrushes

Gray Catbird
Carolina Chickadee
Brown Creeper
Northern Mockingbird
Red-Breasted Nuthatch
White-Breasted Nuthatch

American Robin
Brown Thrasher
Hermit Thrush
Wood Thrush
Carolina Wren
House Wren

Vultures, Hawks, Osprey, and Falcons

Cooper's Hawk
Red-Tailed Hawk
American Kestrel

Osprey
Turkey Vulture

Warblers, Blackbirds, and Tanagers

Yellow-Breasted Chat
Ovenbird
American Restart
Scarlet Tanager
Black-and-White Warbler
Canada Warbler

Hooded Warbler
Pine Warbler
Yellow Warbler
Yellow-Rumped Warbler
Common Yellowthroat

Woodpeckers

Northern Flicker
Yellow-Bellied Sapsucker
Downy Woodpecker

Hairy Woodpecker
Pileated Woodpecker
Red-Bellied Woodpecker

Autumn

Flycatchers, Swallows, Jays, and Crows

American Crow
Fish Crow
Blue Jay
Great-Crested Flycatcher

Eastern Kingbird
Eastern Phoebe
Barn Swallow

Geese and Ducks

American Black Duck
Wood Duck

Canada Goose
Mallards

Goatsuckers

Common Nighthawk

Whip-Poor-Will

Grebes

Double-Crested Cormorant

Grosbeaks, Finches, and Sparrows

Red-Winged Blackbird
Northern Cardinal
Brown-Headed Cowbird
House Finch
Purple Finch

American Goldfinch
Common Grackle
Dark-Eyed Junco
Pine Siskin
House Sparrow

Grouse, Quails, and Turkeys

Northern Bobwhite
Ring-Necked Pheasant

Ruffed Grouse

Herons, Bitterns, and Ibises

Great Blue Heron

Green Heron

Kinglets, Shrikes, and Vireos

Golden-Crowned Kinglet
Ruby-Crowned Kinglet

European Starling
Cedar Waxwing

Kingfishers

Belted Kingfisher

Owls

Barred Owl
Common Barn Owl

Great Horned Owl

Pigeons and Doves

Mourning Dove

Rock Dove

Sandpipers, Gulls, and Terns

Killdeer
Herring Gull
Laughing Gull
Ring-Billed Gull
Spotted Sandpiper

Solitary Sandpiper
Common Snipe
American Woodcock
Greater Yellowlegs
Lesser Yellowlegs

Swifts and Hummingbirds

Ruby-Throated Hummingbird

Titmice, Nuthatches, Wrens, and Mimic Thrushes

Black-Capped Chickadee
Northern Mockingbird
American Robin

Hermit Thrush
Winter Wren

Vultures, Hawks, Ospreys, and Falcons

Peregrine Falcon
Northern Harrier
Cooper's Hawk
Red-Shouldered Hawk
Sharp-Shinned Hawk

American Kestrel
Merlin
Osprey
Turkey Vulture

Warblers, Blackbirds, and Tanagers

Blackpoll
Northern Parula
Bay-Breasted Warbler

Black-and-White Warbler
Black-Throated Blue Warbler
Black-Throated Green Warbler

Cape May Warbler
Chestnut-Sided Warbler
Magnolia Warbler
Nashville Warbler

Palm Warbler
Prairie Warbler
Yellow-Rumped Warbler

Woodpeckers

Northern Flicker
Yellow-Bellied Sapsucker
Downy Woodpecker

Hairy Woodpecker
Red-Bellied Woodpecker

Winter

Grosbeaks, Finches, and Sparrows

Northern Cardinal
House Finch
Purple Finch

American Goldfinch
Evening Grosbeak
Rose-Breasted Grosbeak

Herons

Great Blue Heron

Green Heron

Jays and Crows

American Crow
Fish Crow

Blue Jay

Kingfishers

Belted Kingfisher

Kinglets and Vireos

Eastern Bluebird
Golden-Crowned Kinglet

Ruby-Crowned Kinglet
Cedar Waxwing

Owls

Eastern Screech Owl
Great Horned Owl

Northern Saw-Whet Owl

Pigeons and Doves

Mourning Dove

Rock Dove

Plovers, Sandpipers, and Gulls

Great Black-Backed Gull
Herring Gull
Ring-Billed Gull

Killdeer
American Snipe
American Woodcock

Quails

Northern Bobwhite

Swans, Geese, and Ducks

American Black Duck
Canada Goose
Mallard

Northern Pintail
Tundra Swan

Titmice, Nuthatches, Wrens, and Mimic Thrushes

Black-Capped Chickadee
Brown Creeper
Northern Mockingbird

Red-Breasted Nuthatch
American Robin
Hermit Thrush

House Wren

Winter Wren

Vultures Hawks, Osprey, and Falcons

Northern Harrier
Cooper's Hawk
Sharp-Shinned Hawk
Red-Shouldered Hawk

Red-Tailed Hawk
Rough-Legged Hawk
American Kestrel
Turkey Vulture

Warblers, Blackbirds, and Tanagers

Blackburnian Warbler

Pine Warbler

Woodpeckers

Northern Flicker
Downy Woodpecker

Hairy Woodpecker
Red-Bellied Woodpecker

REPTILES AND AMPHIBIANS

Bullfrog
Gray Tree Frog
Green Frog
Southern Leopard Frog
Wood Frog
Red-Spotted Newt
Northern Spring Peeper
Four-Toed Salamander
Red-Backed Salamander
Black Rate Snake
Eastern Garter Snake
Eastern Milk Snake

Northern Brown (DeKay's) Snake
Northern Water Snake
Eastern Spadefoot
Fowler's Toad
Common Mud Turtle
Common Snapping Turtle
Eastern Box Turtle
Eastern Painted Turtle
Musk Turtle
Red-Bellied Turtle
Spotted Turtle

MAMMALS

Big Brown Bat
Little Brown Bat
Red Bat
Beaver
Chipmunk
Eastern Cottontail
White-Tailed Deer
Gray Fox
Red Fox
Mink
Common Mole
House Mole
Star-Nosed Mole

Meadow Jumping Mouse
White-Footed Mouse
Muskrat
Opossum
Raccoon
Norway Rat
Striped Skunk
Flying Squirrel
Gray Squirrel
Red Squirrel
Meadow Vole
Long-Tailed Weasel
Woodchuck

Cape May: The Jewel in the Crown

If you think of the shape of New Jersey as that of an old man, then Cape May is the "legs" of the state.

It's also the Society's jewel in the crown. Because of its geographical location at the bottom of New Jersey, wedged between the salt marshes of Delaware Bay and the sandy coastline of the Atlantic Ocean—and on the same latitude as Washington, DC—the entire area plays a major role in the spring and fall bird migrations.

As they say, any time of the year is the best time to visit Cape May, although migration months—April and May and late September through early November—are ideal if you want to witness thousands of birds in their migratory travels. These months are also good to catch rare passerines, like the Eurasian widgeon, a duck more commonly seen on the west coast of the United States.

May is also a good time to catch an annual event that draws visitors literally from around the world: the spawning of millions of horseshoe crabs along the Delaware Bay. The crabs are an easy draw for thousands of shorebirds, who fly in to eat the eggs. New Jersey Audubon holds special weekends in May and October. Field trips and lectures are held for everyone, from the simply curious "normal person" to the most advanced birder. The fall weekend exhibition gathers numerous nationally known bird experts, illustrators, and conservationists. The exhibition is free, but bring your wallet, because you'll probably want to buy something—from discounted binoculars and spotting scopes to artworks and books.

Does the Cape offer one bird specialty? No, but raptors and warblers dominate the migration months. The Cape also is a dream-spot for butterfly watchers, offering more than 100 species of butterflies, including the brilliant and plentiful monarch, whose mass migrations are most impressive.

Cape May also offers great white beaches for swimming and sunning, flat roads for jogging and bike-riding, waterways for kayaking and canoeing, trails for hiking and walking, and places to stay and eat for every taste.

New Jersey Audubon has three primary nature centers throughout the cape. Northwood Center at Cape May Point and the Nature Center of Cape May are located at opposite ends of the "Old Man's" toes. The Cape May Bird Observatory Center for Research and Education sits 45 minutes north of the point in Cape May Courthouse, along the Delaware Bayshore. In between are numerous beaches and wildlife management areas that are guaranteed to keep you out of your motel room from dawn until dusk.

We'll start with Northwood Center and the Nature Center, then move up to the Center for Research and Education. After each we'll list numerous areas of interest easily reached from the centers.

Chapter Seven

Northwood Center:
The Naturist Was
a Nature Lover

HISTORY

The Cape May Bird Observatory was founded in 1976, growing out of a bird banding operation begun in 1967 by Bill Clark (who became the observatory's first director). The center made its home in Swansea, the nine-room country home of Anne Ardrey Northwood, widow of naturalist and New Jersey Audubon official J. d'Arcy Northwood.

Strange but true, the gracious widow who donated this small, country home overlooking the point's Lily Lake Pond was as devout a nudist as she was a writer and conservationist. Center officials, who at the time included Clark and a young naturalist named Pete Dunne, quickly moved in, no matter that the lady of the house would reportedly often meet visitors *au naturel*.

Northwood Center
701 East Lake Drive
Cape May Point, NJ
08212
Phone: (609) 884-2736
E-mail: cmbo1@
njaudubon.org

Hours: Daily 10 A.M.
to 5 P.M.

Facilities: Book and
gift store, daily log of
sightings and field trip
schedules, naturalist-
led tours available.

Birding in Cape May

As Dunne, who went on to become the center's program director as well as a nationally known author, once noted, "It's really hard to feel comfortable when a large-boned woman comes out stark naked and tries to sell you her books."

Northwood Center Sign

Northwood died in 1990, leaving the house to New Jersey Audubon.

Anyone visiting Cape May should start the adventure here. The center posts daily activities and sightings outside the front door. The staff here also has on hand two maps that I think are essential to fulfilling your visit: one contains points of interest for all of Cape May County, and the other is for the Delaware

How to Get Here

From all points North and South: Follow the Garden
State Parkway until its end, when it turns into Route
109 South. Continue over two bridges and continue
south down Lafayette Street. At the T-intersection, turn
right for 1.5 miles; this road turns into Sunset
Boulevard. Turn left at Lighthouse Avenue. Turn right
onto East Lake Drive, beyond the center's sign. Parking
is on the road.

Bay shore area. Take two of each; one's bound to fly out an open
window, if you're like me.

There are no trails at the center, but you can visit the bird
feeders and butterfly garden behind the building, and stroll
around the lake to spot various birds, from waterfowl to wood-
cocks and warblers. The center is also a good place to stop for
that extra field guide, pair of binoculars, or baseball cap.

SIDE TRIPS

Returning to Sunset Boulevard, turn right and drive toward
the red-and-white lighthouse
down the road on your left. This
is Cape May Point State Park.
Turn left at the park entrance
(no admission) and follow the
driveway to the parking area.
Park anywhere. You'll see a
sheltered pavilion in front of
you. From here, you can watch
for hawks, shorebirds, and the

Birding the Point

Monarch Banding Demo

occasional pelagic, like shearwaters and petrals. It's also a good place to rest and eat. (Speaking of rest, restrooms are on your right as you enter the park.)

Across the parking lot to your left is the Cape May Hawk Watch. This two-level platform is the formal staging area for the annual hawk watches. It's come a long way since the days when the "platform" was a lifeguard stand. The first formal stand was erected in 1980; it has since been widened and made wheelchair accessible.

Adjacent to the platform is a sheltered picnic area. This too is a good place to stop, rest, and eat.

To the left of the hawk watch platform and shelter is the start to the park's trails. There are three: a half-mile boardwalk trail leading to the point's pond and an observation blind, and two longer trails that thread along the park's phragmites to a second observation deck, then on to sandy paths and the beach.

The trails give you a taste of life in the wetlands. Along the way, you can expect to see numerous wildflowers like the pink and white "marsh mallows" that bear a strong resemblance to hibiscus.

Because of the flat land, all are easy to walk; just take care of the poison ivy that habitually creeps through the boards. If a season has been particularly rainy, it's a good idea to take along a pair of knee-high rubber boots.

From the park, you can make another left on Sunset Boulevard and turn left onto Cape Avenue and proceed to Pavilion Circle Gardens. This little area, sponsored by the

Cape May Point Taxpayers Association, offers a good place to watch for butterflies.

Once finished here, backtrack to Sunset Boulevard and turn right. As you proceed southwest toward the center of Cape May town you come to The Meadows. Of all the places I bird in New Jersey, this is my favorite. Why? For its diversity and its soothing tranquility: By coincidence, I was here Sept. 11, 2001. Within its gentle, mile-loop path is compacted a little bit of every environmental habitat you'll find in

Sunset at Sunset Beach

this part of southern Jersey. You start in a meadow, move onto wetlands, visit a kiss of salt marsh, and follow a gentle slope to

Solitude

the dunes and shoreline. A short walk by the waters, and again you loop down in reverse fashion: visit a kiss of salt marsh, move onto wetlands, end in a meadow.

Along the way, if you're lucky, you'll catch numerous species befitting each environmental type. Cedar waxwings and Cape May warblers flit through in the parking lot; American black ducks, green-winged teals, and mallards can be found in the pond (willets and both lesser and greater yellowlegs come in when the tide's down); least bitterns, green herons, and egrets of all

Brant on the Swim

kinds lurk in the phragmites along the pond edges. From time to time black skimmers come in off the ocean to skim the waters.

The dunes are home to the endangered piping plover. The small birds breed here in the spring. To protect the nests and thumb-sized fledglings, the area is roped off. Birds don't read, so be extra careful even while far off from the nesting area.

Muskrats and water snakes make their home here: Once, I startled a black snake basking along the trail. It scooted into the water as I stood there and, yes, apologized for disturbing it.

Another resident: Poison ivy. If you're going to get a dose while in Cape May, strong chances are you'll get it here. Bring a bottle of Tecnu, just in case.

Another thing: The meadows can flood after heavy rains. Keep your rubber boots in the trunk, just in case. During one summer visit, I forgot mine, and ended up birding in my bare feet. Stepping shoeless in slimy goose effluent is a unique experience.

A short note to photographers: The morning light is too

Northwood Center

harsh for shooting. Wait until late afternoon, when the entire area acquires a rich, golden glow.

From The Meadows, turn right onto Sunset Boulevard and turn left onto Route 607 (Bayshore Road). This will take you to your next stop, The Beanery, a privately

Cygnets at The Meadows

owned working farm. Out of courtesy, please don't walk through the farmlands until you get a sticker from Northwood Center. The sticker is free and promotes good will between the society and The Beanery.

The Beanery trails circle large fields flanked by numerous brush and trees. It's an excellent place for a calming walk or good birding, especially in spring and fall, when warblers and raptors fill the air. Depending on your interests, you can spend an hour or a half-day here.

From here, continue north on Bayshore Road until you come to Hidden Valley. The fields here are comparable to the Beanery, flat and easy to walk, again offering good birding opportunities.

From Hidden Valley, continue north on Bayshore Road until you come to Route 641 (New England Road). Turn left and follow the road until the very end and the sign for Higbee Beach Wildlife Management Area.

"Warblers" and "Higbee Beach" are synonymous among seasoned Cape May birders. The brush and trees bordering the beach's adjoining fields are favorite stopovers for warblers during the spring and fall migration, but you can also find a bevy of hawk activity here as well. During the 2001 fall migration I encountered more merlins, cooper's hawks, kestrels, and sharp-shinneds here than I did while birding from the hawk watch platform at Cape May Point. This is an area where you can spend a full morning birding, if you so choose. An observation deck over the fields lets you better survey the fields.

Because its seclusion invites nude sunbathing, Higbee Beach itself is technically closed to the public in the summer. If you dare to go bare, do so at your own risk and don't tell me!

Chapter Eight

Nature Center
of Cape May:
Backyard Wonders

HISTORY

Wedged between Cape May Harbor and the U.S. Coast Guard training compound, the Nature Center of Cape May was originally the brainchild of the Cape May City Environmental Commission, which established it in 1992. New Jersey Audubon took it over in 1995, and it has been an invaluable facility ever since.

Today, it is a prime environmental education center for youngsters and the young at heart.

The center is a great place to wander around and view its aquarium, which houses various local marine life, or stroll through the small butterfly garden in its backyard.

Nature Center of Cape May

1600 Delaware Avenue
Cape May, NJ 08204
Phone: (609) 898-8848
E-mail: nccm@
njaudubon.org

Hours: Tuesday through Saturday, 10 A.M. to 1 P.M. January through March; Tuesday through Saturday, 10 A.M. to 3 P.M. April through May; daily 9:30 A.M. to 4:30 P.M. June through September; Tuesday through Saturday, 10 A.M. to 3 P.M. October through December.

Facilities: Indoor/outdoor classrooms, aquaria, butterfly garden, visitor center, and gift shop. Educational programs for children and adults that include workshops, field trips, and other programs are offered throughout the year.

The Nature Center

Purple Martin Houses

How to Get Here

From all points North: Take the Garden State Parkway south to the end and keep going south once the highway turns into Route 109. Cross two bridges, then make a left onto Sydney Avenue. Turn left at the stop sign and make the next right onto Texas Avenue. Proceed to Delaware Avenue and turn left. Delaware Avenue is under the yellow blinking light.

Hint: You can also just follow the signs for the Coast Guard Training Academy.

From the South: To get from the more southern parts of Cape May, take Sunset Boulevard east and turn right onto Broadway. Turn left onto Beach Drive. Drive through town and make a left onto Pittsburgh Avenue and continue on to Delaware, which will be after the yellow blinking light. Turn right. The center is two blocks down.

SIDE TRIPS

Between Cape May Point and the Education and Research Center are numerous other areas of interest. Retrace your steps up the Parkway North to Exit 4 and follow the signs to Rio Grande and Route 47 North. Norbury's Landing, and Kimble's, Cook's, and Reed's beaches are excellent spots to watch the horseshoe crabs during the season. Bring your camera and spotting scope, but be sure to keep your distance from the beaches and use the observation platforms.

You may also want to stop at the Cape May National Wildlife Refuge. Headquarters is off Kimble's Beach Road. Stop here for information. You can also park on Woodcock Lane and take the trail, which takes you through fields and forests for a good look at migrants.

Farther up North 47 you'll find the Goshen Landing. Take a left at the Goshen Post Office and follow the road, which can turn muddy in rainy weather. There are salt marsh pools here where you can catch a good look at the purple Glossy Ibis. Continuing north on the highway will take you to the Cape May Bird Observatory Center for Research and Education.

Chapter Nine

CMBO Center for Research and Education: Butterflies 'R Us

TERRAIN

Located 45 minutes north of Northwood Center, on the Delaware Bay shore side, CMBO's Center for Research and Education is surrounded by 26 acres of marshes and upland topography that offer visitors a nice wildlife diversity. Its butterfly gardens invite a brilliant rainbow of butterflies during the summer months, including Monarchs, whose mass migration is a high point of the center's year. Ruby-throated hummingbirds also frequent the center's feeders and flowers, and can amuse visitors with their feeding antics and chattering for hours on end.

CMBO Center for Research and Education
600 Route 47 North
Cape May Court
House, NJ 08210
Phone: (609) 861-0700
E-mail: cmbo2@
njaudubon.org

Hours: Daily 10 A.M.
to 5 P.M.

Facilities: Book and
gift shop, an upstairs
loft/gallery for photography and art exhibits,
field trips, and educational programs for
children and adults.

Nature Center

TRAILS

The small trail around
the center leads beyond
the butterfly gardens and
pond through a meadow
that looks out onto
nearby wetlands. From
here, visitors can often
catch glimpses of egrets
and herons, plus the
occasional bittern if you
look closely enough.

Garden Trail, Center for
Education and Research

How to Get Here

From all directions North: Take the Garden State Parkway south to Exit 13 and turn right. Proceed to the light and turn left onto Route 9 South. Turn right onto Route 646 until you reach Route 47. Turn right and proceed south for a little more than a mile and a half. The center will be on your right.

Another option is to take the Garden State Parkway south to Exit 10 and turn right there. From here, you proceed straight until you reach Route 47. Turn left onto the highway and proceed south. The center is about a mile down on your left.

From the South: You have two options: Take the Parkway up to Exit 4 and follow the Rio Grande ramp to Route 47 north, continuing to areas of interest mentioned previously. Or, you can proceed north on the Parkway to Exit 10. Turn left at the exit and proceed straight until you reach Route 47. Turn left onto the highway and proceed about a mile to the center.

SIDE TRIPS

Visiting the New Jersey Audubon nature centers at Cape May is just the start of your fun in this area. There are numerous places to walk, or bird, or even paddle. These spots can be divided into those on the Bayshore side, and those on the ocean side.

Since we're already discussing the Bayshore area, we'll start with places of interest you can visit after leaving the center at Goshen.

Bayshore Side

Goshen is an excellent starting point for other areas of natural interest up and down the Bayshore. Before traveling on to these it would also be a good idea to use the center's facilities, especially in the summer months: You do not need to run into the woods only to be plagued by pesky strawberry flies.

Below are just a handful of side trips you can take. Depending on your schedule, these can be done in a half or full day.

Leaving the Education and Research Center, turn left onto Route 47 and proceed through North Dennis. Jake's Landing will be on your left. Be careful: The street sign is small, but there is a boat launch sign. Turn left onto Jake's Landing Road and just drive to the end.

More formally known as the Dennis Creek Wildlife Management Area, Jake's Landing is an excellent spot to look for pine and yellow-throated warblers and woodland butterflies. You can also put in for some canoeing or kayaking through the area's tidal marshes. (*Note*: Tides are strong. Be sure you have a schedule of tides for the area and plan accordingly.) As you paddle the waters you can get a good eyeful of egrets and herons. If you're lucky, you'll catch sight of the elusive clapper rail.

If you don't have a boat to float, catch the wildlife from the

observation platform.

Leaving Jake's Landing, proceed down the road and again turn left. Proceed north on Route 47 until you come to Stipson's Island Road.

Monarch Butterfly

Formerly known as the Dennis Township Wetland Restoration Site, this 560-acre site, purchased by a local utility company to promote fish productivity, offers another great view of life in the coastal tidal marshes. Bald eagles and northern harriers can often be seen perched or hovering over the fields, and, when the winds are right, black skimmers fly in off the bay in search of food. Seaside sparrows make their home here, too, as do herons and clapper rails.

Sedum

Visitors can walk the short, descriptive boardwalk or, again, put in at the boat ramp.

From Stipson's Island, return to Route 47 and turn left. A stone's throw away on your right is the Eldora Nature Preserve. The preserve offers interpretive exhibits, aquaria, gift shop, and butterfly and hummingbird gardens. A nature trail takes you through woodlands to the marsh.

When finished here, turn right on Route 47 and head north. You will leave Cape May County and enter Cumberland County. Turn left onto Route 616 and follow the signs to the Heislerville Wildlife Management Area and an eight-mile wildlife viewing drive that lets you scout out the Maurice River and its surrounding mud flats. I've seen numerous types of shorebirds here, as well as several green herons.

Maurice River Park can be accessed from Route 47 by taking Route 670 (watch for the Wawa and Campbell's Market on the corner). Bald eagles and other raptors can be seen from viewpoints around the bridge. An early migration of thousands of purple martins in late August/early September is the big highlight here.

Unless you care to continue north up Route 47 into Cumberland and Salem counties—an excursion that can take you two and a half hours away from Cape May—you may just want to turn back. A final side trip to Belleplain State Forest could net many warblers, butterflies, and some good hiking trails. To get there, continue south on Route 47 below Eldora and turn west onto Route 557. Turn north onto 550 and proceed to the park. You can get a map and use the facilities at the park's field office.

Ocean Side

Cape May's Atlantic coast offers its own variations of birds and waterfowl. Start with the Hereford Inlet Lighthouse Gardens in North Wildwood. To get there, drive north on the Garden State Parkway to Exit 6 and follow the signs to the beachfront. Turn onto First Avenue to Central Avenue until you come to the lighthouse. The gardens surround the lighthouse. This area is particularly good in the fall for migrants, and for summer butterflies. You can get a good view of Champagne Island from here, but a scope is helpful.

From the gardens, retrace your steps to the Parkway and proceed north to Exit 10; turn right and follow the signs to Stone Harbor, an upbeat, trendy seaside resort, which has grown in size and popularity lately. As you drive along Stone Harbor Boulevard, you'll pass a number of marsh and salt ponds; the nonprofit Wetlands Institute to your right offers a boardwalk from which you could observe nesting ospreys in the spring. As you enter Stone Harbor itself, turn right at the second light onto 2nd Avenue and proceed all the way to the end, which is 122nd Street. There's a parking lot on the left. This is another spot that's good for fall migrants and butterflies.

If you drive south from here, a small bridge will take you to Nummy's Island, another spot that provides good birding.

If you're in Cape May during fall migration, take Exit 13 off the Parkway and proceed into Avalon to 7th Street, where CMBO holds a sea watch.

On your return trip north from Cape May, you may also want to consider taking in the eight-mile drive/walk of the Forsythe National Wildlife Refuge, more commonly called Brigantine. Again, the refuge, from where you also gets a bird's eye view of the Atlantic City skyline, offers great walking and birding throughout the year.

To get to Brigantine, take the Garden State Parkway north to the Exit 41 service area and turn right at Great Creek Road. Continue on, crossing Route 9, until you see the refuge sign.

BIRDS

Note: The following list encompasses all Cape May birding areas. Birds listed are those commonly seen during the seasons indicated.

Spring

Bitterns to Vultures

American Bittern	Black-Crowned Night Heron
Least Bittern	Great Blue Heron
Great Egret	Black Vultures
Snowy Egret	Turkey Vultures

Blackbirds and Old World Sparrows

Bobolink	Boat-Tailed Grackle
Red-Winged Blackbird	Common Grackle
Brown-Headed Cowbird	Eastern Meadowlark
House Finch	Baltimore Oriole
American Goldfinch	Orchard Oriole

Coots and Rails

American Coot   Clapper Rail

Gulls, Terns, and Skimmers

Bonaparte's Gull   Black Skimmer
Great Black-Backed Gull   Common Tern
Herring Gull   Forster's Tern
Laughing Gull   Royal Tern
Ring-Billed Gull

Jays to Wrens

Carolina Chickadee   Barn Swallow
American Crow   Tree Swallow
Fish Crow   Tufted Titmouse
Blue Jay   Carolina Wren
Purple Martin   House Wren
Bank Swallow   Marsh Wren

Kinglets to Waxwings

Gray Catbird   European Starling
Blue-Gray Gnatcatcher   Brown Thrasher
Golden-Crowned Kinglet   Hermit Thrush
Ruby-Crowned Kinglet   Wood Thrush
Northern Mockingbird   Cedar Waxwing
American Robin

Loons to Cormorants

Double-Crested Cormorant   Common Loon
Northern Gannet   Red-Throated Loon
Horned Grebe

Pigeons to Woodpeckers

Mourning Dover
Rock Dove
Northern Flicker
Ruby-Throated Hummingbird
Chimney Swift

Chuck-Will's-Widow
Whip-Poor-Will
Downy Woodpecker
Red-Bellied Woodpecker

Raptors

Osprey
Northern Harrier
Broad-Winged Hawk

Red-Tailed Hawk
American Kestrel
Eastern Screech Owl

Shorebirds

American Oyster Catcher
Short-Billed Dowitcher
Dunlin
Killdeer
Red Knot
Black-Bellied Plover
Semipalmated Plover
Sanderling
Least Sandpiper

Purple Sandpiper
Semipalmated Sandpiper
Spotted Sandpiper
Common Snipe
Ruddy Turnstone
Whimbrel
Willet
Lesser Yellowlegs

Tanagers to Buntings

Indigo Bunting
Dark-Eyed Junco
Blue Grosbeak
Rose-Breasted Grosbeak
Chipping Sparrow
Field Sparrow
Saltmarsh Sharp-Tailed Sparrow

Savannah Sparrow
Seaside Sparrow
Song Sparrow
Swamp Sparrow
Scarlet Tanager
Eastern Towhee

Warblers

Blackpoll
Yellow-Breasted Chat
Ovenbird
Northern Parula
American Redstart
Black-Throated Blue Warbler
Black-and-White Warbler
Blue-Winged Warbler

Magnolia Warbler
Pine Warbler
Prairie Warbler
Prothonotary Warbler
Worm-Eating Warbler
Yellow Warbler
Yellow-Rumped Warbler
Common Yellowthroat

Waterfowl

Brant
Bufflehead
Canada Goose
Snow Goose
Common Goldeneye
American Black Duck
Wood Duck
Gadwall
Mallard
Red-Breasted Merganser
Northern Pintail

Oldsquaw
Greater Scaup
Lesser Scaup
Black Scoter
Surf Scoter
Northern Shovetail
Mute Swan
Blue-Winged Teal
Green-Winged Teal
American Wigeon

Summer

Blackbirds to Old World Sparrows

Red-Winged Blackbird
Brown-Headed Cowbird
House Finch
American Goldfinch

Boat-Tailed Grackle
Common Grackle
Orchard Oriole
House Sparrow

Bitterns to Vultures

American Bittern
Least Bittern
Great Egret
Snowy Egret

Black-Crowned Night Heron
Green Heron
Glossy Ibis
Turkey Vulture

Flycatchers to Vireos

Acadian Flycatcher
Great-Crested Flycatcher
Eastern Kingbird

Eastern Wood Peewee
Red-Eyed Vireo
White-Eyed Vireo

Gulls, Terns, and Skimmers

Great Black-Backed Gull
Herring Gull
Laughing Gull
Black Skimmer

Common Tern
Forster's Tern
Least Tern

Jays to Wrens

Carolina Chickadee
American Crow
Fish Crow
Blue Jay
Purple Martin
Barn Swallow

Tree Swallow
Tufted Titmouse
Carolina Wren
House Wren
Marsh Wren

Kinglets to Waxwings

Gray Catbird
Blue-Gray Gnatcatcher
Northern Mockingbird
American Robin

European Starling
Wood Thrush
Cedar Waxwing

Loons to Cormorants

Double-Crested Cormorants

Pigeons to Woodpeckers

Mourning Dove
Rock Dove
Northern Flicker
Ruby-Throated Hummingbird

Chimney Swift
Chuck-Will's-Widow
Whip-Poor-Will
Downy Woodpecker

Rails

Clapper Rail

Raptors

Osprey

Eastern Screech Owl

Shorebirds

Short-Billed Dowitcher
Red Knot
American Oystercatcher

Sanderling
Willet

Tanagers to Buntings

Indigo Bunting
Northern Cardinal
Blue Grosbeak
Chipping Sparrow
Field Sparrow
Saltmarsh Sharp-Tailed Sparrow

Seaside Sparrow
Song Sparrow
Swamp Sparrow
Scarlet Tanager
Eastern Towhee

Warblers

Yellow-Breasted Chat
Ovenbird
Black-and-White Warbler
Blue-Winged Warbler
Pine Warbler

Prairie Warbler
Prothonotary Warbler
Yellow Warbler
Yellow-Throated Warbler
Common Yellowthroat

Waterfowl

American Black Duck
Canada Goose

Mallard
Mute Swan

Autumn

Blackbirds to Old World Sparrows

Red-Winged Blackbird
Bobolink
Brown-Headed Catbird
House Finch
American Goldfinch

Boat-Tailed Grackle
Common Grackle
Eastern Meadowlark
Baltimore Oriole
House Sparrow

Egrets to Vultures

Cattle Egret
Great Egret
Snowy Egret
Black-Crowned Night Heron
Great Blue Heron

Little Blue Heron
Tricolored Heron
Glossy Ibis
Black Vulture
Turkey Vulture

Flycatchers to Vireos

Great-Crested Flycatcher
Eastern Wood Peewee

Red-Eyed Vireo

Gulls, Terns, and Skimmers

Bonaparte's Gull
Great Black-Backed Gull
Herring Gull
Laughing Gull
Ring-Billed Gull

Black Skimmer
Common Tern
Forster's Tern
Royal Tern

Jays to Wrens

Carolina Chickadee
American Crow
Fish Crow
Blue Jay
Purple Martin
Red-Breasted Nuthatch

Barn Swallow
Tree Swallow
Tufted Titmouse
Carolina Wren
Marsh Wren

Kinglets to Waxwings

Eastern Bluebird
Gray Catbird
Blue-Gray Gnatcatcher
Golden-Crowned Kinglet
Ruby-Crowned Kinglet

Northern Mockingbird
American Robin
European Starling
Hermit Thrush
Cedar Waxwing

Loons to Cormorants

Double-Crested Cormorant
Northern Gannet
Horned Grebe

Pied-Billed Grebe
Common Loon
Red-Throated Loon

Pigeons to Woodpeckers

Mourning Dove
Rock Dove
Northern Flicker
Ruby-Throated Hummingbird

Chimney Swift
Downy Woodpecker
Red-Bellied Woodpecker

Rails and Coots

American Coot

Clapper Rail

Raptors

Bald Eagle
Peregrine Falcon
Northern Harrier
Broad-Winged Hawk
Cooper's Hawk
Red-Shouldered Hawk

Red-Tailed Hawk
Sharp-Shinned Hawk
American Kestrel
Merlin
Osprey
Eastern Screech Owl

Shorebirds

Short-Billed Dowitcher
Dunlin
Black-Bellied Plover
Semipalmated Plover
Killdeer
American Oystercatcher
Sanderling
Least Sandpiper
Pectoral Sandpiper
Purple Sandpiper
Semipalmated Sandpiper

Spotted Sandpiper
Stilted Sandpiper
Western Sandpiper
White-Rumped Sandpiper
Common Snipe
Ruddy Turnstone
Whimbrel
Willet
American Woodcock
Greater Yellowlegs
Lesser Yellowlegs

Tanagers to Buntings

Indigo Bunting
Northern Cardinal
Blue Grosbeak
Dark-Eyed Junco
Chipping Sparrow
Field Sparrow
Savannah Sparrow

Saltmarsh Sharp-Tailed Sparrow
Seaside Sparrow
Song Sparrow
Swamp Sparrow
White-Throated Sparrow
Scarlet Tanager
Eastern Towhee

Warblers

Blackpoll
Ovenbird
Northern Parula
American Redstart
Black-Throated Blue Warbler
Black-Throated Green Warbler
Blackburnian Warbler
Blue-Winged Warbler
Canada Warbler
Cape May Warbler
Magnolia Warbler

Nashville Warbler
Palm Warbler
Pine Warbler
Prairie Warbler
Worm-Eating Warbler
Yellow Warbler
Yellow-Rumped Warbler
Yellow-Throated Warbler
Northern Waterthrush
Common Yellowthroat

Waterfowl

Bufflehead
American Black Duck
Wood Duck
Gadwall
Common Goldeneye
Canada Goose
Snow Goose
Mallard
Hooded Merganser
Red-Breasted Merganser
Oldsquaw

Northern Pintail
Greater Scaup
Lesser Scaup
Surf Scoter
Northern Shoveler
Mute Swan
Tundra Swan
Blue-Winged Teal
Green-Winged Teal
American Wigeon

Winter

Blackbirds to Old World Sparrows

Red-Winged Blackbird
House Finch
American Goldfinch
Boat-Tailed Grackle

Brown-Headed Grackle
Common Grackle
Eastern Meadowlark
House Sparrow

Coots

American Coot

Gulls

Bonaparte's Gull
Great Black-Backed Gull

Herring Gull
Ring-Billed Gull

Herons and Vultures

Great Blue Heron
Black Vulture

Turkey Vulture

Jays to Wrens

Carolina Chickadee
American Crow
Fish Crow

Blue Jay
Tufted Titmouse
Carolina Wren

Kinglets to Waxwings

Northern Mockingbird
American Robin

European Starling
Cedar Waxwing

Loons and Grebes

Northern Gannet
Horned Grebe
Pied-Billed Grebe

Common Loon
Red-Throated Loon

Pigeons to Woodpeckers

Mourning Dove
Rock Dove
Northern Flicker

Downy Woodpecker
Red-Bellied Woodpecker

Raptors

Northern Harrier
Red-Tailed Hawk

Eastern Screech Owl

Shorebirds

Dunlin
Killdeer
American Oystercatcher
Black-Bellied Plover

Sanderling
Purple Sandpiper
Western Sandpiper
Ruddy Turnstone

Tanagers to Buntings

Northern Cardinal
Dark-Eyed Junco
Song Sparrow

Swamp Sparrow
White-Throated Sparrow

Warblers

Yellow-Rumped Warbler

Waterfowl

Brant
Bufflehead
American Black Duck
Gadwall
Common Goldeneye
Canada Goose
Snow Goose
Mallard
Hooded Merganser
Red-Breasted Merganser

Oldsquaw
Northern Pintail
Greater Scaup
Lesser Scaup
Black Scoter
Surf Scoter
White-Winged Scoter
Northern Shoveler
Green-Winged Teal
American Wigeon

BUTTERFLIES

Early Spring (Late March to Mid-May)

Brushfoots

Red Admiral
Mourning Cloak
Eastern Comma
Pearl Crescent
Meadow Fritillary

Silver-Bordered Fritillary
American Lady
Painted Lady
Question Mark
Compton Tortoiseshell

Harvesters, Coppers, Hairstreaks, and Blues

Coastal Holly Azure
"Northern" Spring Azure
Eastern Tailed Blue
American Copper
Brown Elfin
Eastern Pine Elfin
Frosted Elfin

Henry's Elfin
Gray Hairstreak
Hessel's Hairstreak
"Olive" Juniper Hairstreak
Red-Banded Hairstreak
White M Hairstreak

Milkweed Butterflies

Monarch

Skippers

Horace's Duskywing
Juvenal's Duskywing
Sleepy Duskywing

Wild Indigo Duskywing
Cobweb Skipper
Silver-Spotted Skipper

Swallowtails

Black Swallowtail

E. Tiger Swallowtail

Spicebush Swallowtail

Zebra Swallowtail

Whites and Sulphurs

Clouded Sulphur
Orange Sulphur
Falcate Orange Tip

Cabbage White
Checkered White

Additional Species

Hoary Elfin

Late Spring (Mid-May to Mid-June)

Brushfoots

Red Admiral
Common Buckeye
Mourning Cloak
Eastern Comma
Pearl Crescent
Variegated Fritillary

American Lady
Painted Lady
Question Mark
Red-Spotted Purple
Viceroy

Hackberry Butterflies

Hackberry Emperor

Tawny Emperor

Harvesters, Coppers, Hairstreaks, and Blues

Coastal Holly Azure
Summer Azure
Eastern Tailed Blue
American Copper
Eastern Pine Elfin

Frosted Elfin
Gray Hairstreak
Red-Banded Hairstreak
White M Hairstreak
Harvester

Milkweed Butterflies

Monarch

Satyrs and Wood Nymphs

Little Wood Satyr

Skippers

Northern Cloudywing
Southern Cloudywing
Horace's Duskywing
Juvenal's Duskywing
Sleepy Duskywing
Wild Indigo Duskywing
Hoary Edge
Little Glassywing
Sachem
Hayhurst's Scallopwing
Aaron's Skipper
Cobweb Skipper
Common Roadside Skipper

Crossline Skipper
Delaware Skipper
Dun Skipper
Dusted Skipper
European Skipper
Least Skipper
Peck's Skipper
Salt Marsh Skipper
Silver-Spotted Skipper
Swarthy Skipper
Tawny-Edged Skipper
Zabulon Skipper
Common Sootywing

Snouts

American Snout

Swallowtails

Black Swallowtail
E. Tiger Swallowtail

Spicebush Swallowtail
Zebra Swallowtail

Whites and Sulphurs

Clouded Sulphur
Cloudless Sulphur
Orange Sulphur

Cabbage White
Checkered White

Additional Species

Confused Cloudywing
Golden-Banded Skipper

Hobomok Skipper
Indian Skipper

Early Summer (Mid-June to Mid-July)

Brushfoots

Red Admiral
Baltimore
Common Buckeye
Mourning Cloak
Eastern Comma
Pearl Crescent
American Lady
Painted Lady
Aphrodite Fritillary

Great-Spangled Fritillary
Meadow Fritillary
Silver-Bordered Fritillary
Variegated Fritillary
Question Mark
Red-Spotted Purple
Compton Tortoiseshell
Viceroy

Hackberry Butterflies

Hackberry Emperor

Tawny Emperor

Harvesters, Coppers, Hairstreaks, and Blues

Summer Azure
Eastern Tailed Blue
American Copper
Bog Copper
Bronze Copper
Banded Hairstreak
Coral Hairstreak

Gray Hairstreak
"Olive" Juniper Hairstreak
Red-Banded Hairstreak
Southern Hairstreak
Striped Hairstreak
Harvester

Milkweed Butterflies

Monarch

Satyrs and Wood Nymphs

Appalachian Brown
Eyed Brown

Common Wood Nymph
Georgia Satyr

Skippers

Northern Cloudywing
Southern Cloudywing
Black Dash
Horace's Duskywing
Wild Indigo Duskywing
Zarucco Duskywing
Hoary Edge
Little Glassywing
Sachem
Hayhurst's Scallopwing
Aaron's Skipper
Broad-Winged Skipper
Common Checkered Skipper
Crossline Skipper

Delaware Skipper
Dun Skipper
European Skipper
Least Skipper
Rare Skipper
Salt Marsh Skipper
Silver-Spotted Skipper
Swarthy Skipper
Tawny-Edged Skipper
Two-Spotted Skipper
Zabulon Skipper
Common Sootywing
Mulberry Wing

Snouts

American Snout

Swallowtails

Black Swallowtail
E. Tiger Swallowtail
Pipevine Swallowtail

Spicebush Swallowtail
Zebra Swallowtail

Whites and Sulphurs

Clouded Sulphur
Cloudless Sulphur
Orange Sulphur

Cabbage White
Checkered White

Additional Species

Confused Cloudywing
Edward's Hairstreak
Arogos Skipper

Dotted Skipper
Hobomok Skipper

Mid-Summer (Mid-July to Late August)

Brushfoots

Red Admiral
Common Buckeye
Mourning Cloak
Eastern Comma
Gray Comma
Pearl Crescent
Aphrodite Fritillary

Great Spangled Fritillary
Variegated Fritillary
American Lady
Painted Lady
Question Mark
Red-Spotted Purple
Viceroy

Harvesters, Coppers, Hairstreaks, and Blues

Summer Azure
Eastern Tailed Blue
American Copper
Bronze Copper
Gray Hairstreak

"Olive" Juniper Hairstreak
Red-Banded Hairstreak
White M Hairstreak
Harvester

Hackberry Butterflies

Hackberry Emperor

Tawny Emperor

Milkweed Butterflies

Monarch

Satyrs and Wood Nymphs

Appalachian Brown
Eyed Brown
Common Wood Nymph

Georgia Satyr
Little Wood Satyr

Skippers

Northern Cloudywing
Southern Cloudywing
Northern Broken Dash
Horace's Duskywing
Wild Indigo Duskywing
Zarucco Duskywing
Hayhurst's Scallopwing
Aaron's Skipper
Broad-Winged Skipper
Clouded Skipper
Common Checkered Skipper
Common Roadside Skipper
Crossline Skipper

Delaware Skipper
Dun Skipper
Fiery Skipper
Least Skipper
Peck's Skipper
Rare Skipper
Salt Marsh Skipper
Silver-Spotted Skipper
Swarthy Skipper
Tawny-Edged Skipper
Zabulon Skipper
Common Sootywing
Whirlabout

Snouts

American Snout

Swallowtails

Black Swallowtail
E. Tiger Swallowtail
Pipevine Swallowtail

Spicebush Swallowtail
Zebra Swallowtail

Whites and Sulphurs

Sleepy Orange
Clouded Sulphur
Cloudless Sulphur
Orange Sulphur

Cabbage White
Checkered White
Little Yellow

Additional Species

Confused Cloudywing
Arogos Skipper

Dotted Skipper

Late Summer/Autumn (September to October/November)

Brushfoots

Red Admiral
Common Buckeye
Mourning Cloak
Eastern Comma
Gray Comma
Pear Crescent
Great Spangled Fritillary
Gulf Fritillary
Meadow Fritillary

Regal Fritillary
Silver-Bordered Fritillary
Variegated Fritillary
American Lady
Painted Lady
Question Mark
Red-Spotted Purple
Compton Tortoiseshell
Viceroy

Hackberry Butterflies

Hackberry Emperor

Tawny Emperor

Harvesters, Coppers, Hairstreaks, and Blues

Summer Azure
Eastern Tailed Blue
American Copper
Bronze Copper
Gray Hairstreak

Great Purple Hairstreak
Red-Banded Hairstreak
White M Hairstreak
Harvester

Milkweed Butterflies

Monarch

Satyrs and Wood Nymphs

Common Wood Nymph

Skippers

Southern Cloudywing
Horace's Duskywing
Wild Indigo Duskywing
Zarucco Duskywing
Sachem
Hayhurst's Scallopwing
Common Sootywing
Aaron's Skipper
Brazilian Skipper
Clouded Skipper
Common Checkered Skipper
Crossline Skipper
Eufala Skipper

Fiery Skipper
Least Skipper
Leonard's Skipper
Long-Tailed Skipper
Ocola Skipper
Peck's Skipper
Salt Marsh Skipper
Silver-Spotted Skipper
Swarthy Skipper
Tawny-Edged Skipper
Zabulon Skipper
Whirlabout

Snouts

American Snout

Swallowtails

Black Swallowtail
E. Tiger Swallowtail
Palamedes Swallowtail

Pipevine Swallowtail
Spicebush Swallowtail

Whites and Sulphurs

Sleepy Orange
Clouded Sulphur
Cloudless Sulphur
Orange Sulphur

Cabbage White
Checkered White
Little Yellow

Additional Species

Confused Cloudywing
Southern Dogface

Orange-Barred Sulphur
Giant Swallowtail

WILDFLOWERS

Amsonia
Arrowwood
New England Aster
Butterfly Bush
Catmint
Black Chokeberry
Moonbeam Coreopsis
Marjorem
Hummingbird Mint
Nannyberry

Phlox
English Plantain
Flowering Quince
Salvia
Scarlet Sage
Sedum
Mexican Sunflower
Perennial Sunflower
Brazilian Verbana
Cranberry Viburnum

Part 2

The Preserves: Fun Off the Beaten Path

New Jersey Audubon has numerous preserves throughout the state. Many of these properties have been deeded or given to the society over the years for the purpose of conservation, and to ensure that environmentally sensitive properties are not gobbled up by development.

While many of these preserves are not accessible to the public, the following are. Like the staffed nature centers, they are located throughout the state, from the Highlands to Cape May's coastal plains.

Remember, these areas are not staffed. In most cases, there are no facilities. Since the preserves are monitored by the appropriate nature center, you may want to call ahead to check conditions and to request a trail map.

As with the staffed centers, this section starts with the Highlands, and Sparta Mountain.

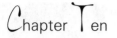

Chapter Ten

Sparta Mountain: Highlands Fun

TRAILS

Like the trails at the Weis Ecology Center, Sparta Mountain offers the best of the New Jersey Highlands: wild and wooly trails whose forests and brush define the term "woods." Dense and steep in parts, the trails take visitors past waterfalls and wetlands.

The preserve is adjacent to some 1,400 acres managed by both New Jersey and the state Fish and Game service.

There are two entrances. One trail entrance sits on Edison Road near the turn off Glen Road: Watch for the brown New Jersey Audubon sign on the right. Another entrance is farther up Edison Road near the monument of Thomas Edison. All trails are marked.

The first trail of Edison Road parallels the road leading to Ryker Lake, a small lake that's a favorite for trout anglers in the spring. From here, a trail loops deeper into

Sparta Mountain

Sparta and Hardyston,
Sussex County and
Jefferson Township,
Morris County

349 acres

For information,
contact Scherman-
Hoffman Wildlife
Sanctuary, (908) 766-
5787

Hours: Dawn to dusk
year-round

Best times to visit:
May and early June
for warblers; October
and November for fall
birding

No facilities.

Edison Monument

the woods, taking visi-
tors over a stream and
cascading waterfall. A
connecting trail leads
from the lake up the
Highlands Trail.

The second trail
entrance is at the statue

Falls, Sparta Mountain

How to Get Here

From the North: Take Route 23 South to Berkshire Valley Road. Make a left onto Ridge Road, which turns into Glen Road. Continue to Edison Road and turn right. Parking is available.

From the South: Take Route 23 North to Berkshire Valley Road. Make a right onto Ridge Road, which turns into Glen Road. Follow the above directions.

From the East: Take Route 80 West to Route 23 North and follow above directions.

From the West: Take Route 80 East to Route 287 to Route 23 North. Follow above directions.

of Thomas Edison. A short trail loops behind the statue passing an 18th-century mill race and a sinkhole, which someone has memorialized with a makeshift monument indicating the hole has a depth of 86 feet.

From the loop trail, you can either circle back to the monument, or continue on to the Highlands Trail.

Trail access is also available about one and a half miles north of a new home development on Edison Road.

Lambs' Ear, Sparta Mountain

Chapter Eleven

Old Farm Sanctuary:
43 Species in an Hour

Nestled in the southwestern edge of the Highlands in rural Warren County, Old Farm Sanctuary is actually comprised of two sanctuaries: the Remley sanctuary, a 99-acre tract that runs through rugged hills to a ridgetop; and the gentler, ambling Stramaglia sanctuary contiguously located at the base of the ridge.

Remley was donated by Evelyn Remley in 1991; the smaller Stramaglia portion was donated in 1994, when Frank Stramaglia donated a 50-acre tract in the memory of his parents, Frank, Sr. and Josephine.

Although only 151 aces, Old Farm terrain is delightfully diverse and representative of the numerous types of terrain experienced in northwest New Jersey. While situated in the Highlands, the area has the typical Highlands characteristics of woods and ridges, but at the same time has wetlands and meadows, terrain consistent with the

Old Farm Sanctuary
Independence
Township, New Jersey

151 acres

For information,
contact Scherman-
Hoffman Wildlife
Sanctuary, (908) 766-
5878

Hours: Dawn to dusk
year-round

Best times to visit:
May (warblers and
butterflies), early June;
October and
November for fall
birding in Stramaglia
section.

No facilities. Picnic
tables in Stramaglia
Sanctuary section.

Old Farm Sanctuary, Stramaglia entrance

sloping Piedmont area. Remley, the upper sanctuary, is mostly rugged forest. Stramaglia, the lower sanctuary, is all wetlands and meadows.

Old Farm Sanctuary is small enough that visitors can manage to visit one or both of the properties in one day.

Because of the terrain diversity, a full complement of bird species can be found. These species include herons, raptors, woodpeckers, and a variety of songbirds. Most of these birds can be found breeding in the spring.

In 1991, when Remley donated her property, New Jersey Audubon officials strolled through her property and counted 43 species—all in the first hour they were there.

Trees include tulip poplars, red maples, red oaks, black tupelo, sweet birch, and dogwoods in lower areas; tulip poplar, red cedar,

How to Get Here

From North and South: Take Route 287 to the Route 80 West exit. Proceed to Exit 19 and Route 517. Take a left onto Route 517 and proceed toward Hackettstown. Turn right at Route 46 and proceed west through the town to Route 614 (Petersburg Road). Follow Petersburg Road until you come to a "Y" fork: A red barn will be in the middle of the fork. Here you have two options: You can follow the road to the right (Ryan Road) and proceed a short distance up the hill to the Remley sanctuary parking lot on your left, or you can take the left fork (Water Street) and proceed a short distance to the Stramaglia sanctuary and the parking lot on your right.

white ash, red oak on the slope; hickory and oaks on the ridge; Norway spruce and sugar maples.

Plants include squawroot, one-flowered cankerroot, violet wood sorrel, Virginia snakeroot, white beard-tongue, maidenhair fern, and rattlesnake fern.

TRAILS

Remley Sanctuary

The Remley sanctuary offers three trail options. The Short Loop takes you up a short flight of steps into the woods, then to a short trail that loops about a quarter mile from the parking lot and back. The only climbing here is up the steps, and there is a small slope that leads onto the sanctuary's dirt road, which was once the real Ryan Road.

Your second option, the Long Loop, leads you from the parking lot up the steps but onto a longer section of trail that takes

Old Farm Trail

you through the woods eventually to the "edge" area of the woods. The edge breaks out into the Old Farm meadow. To the south of the fields runs a stream named Bacon Run.

From the meadow you can circle back to the parking lot, or proceed to Overlook Trail. This is a particularly challenging trail that leads you from the Long Loop straight up a 550-foot incline that is relatively challenging, taking you up and down a rocky trail that ends with a spectacular view of the area, which is excellent for hawk-watching, especially during the spring and fall migration seasons. If you take this trail, make sure your hiking shoes or boots have traction; a walking stick can also help.

On your return from the Overlook, you have the option of following the Long Loop back to the parking lot, or following the loop until it connects with the trail that leads from the meadow to the flatter, more genteel Stramaglia Sanctuary.

Stramaglia Sanctuary

Stramaglia is a hiker's rest haven. The easy trail from the parking lot passes through wetlands terrain filled with deciduous trees and a stream before connecting with the Remley sanctuary trails in the Old Farm meadow. Virginia creeper lines the narrow path, as do dogwoods, whose red berries in fall attract scores of cedar waxwings. This is also a good area to view neotropicals throughout the year, especially Blackburnian warblers.

Of particular interest along the way is the Norway spruce grove, where red squirrels can often be found noshing pinecones.

Should you grow tired or hungry in Stramaglia, you have the luxury of pausing at one of three picnic groves.

One word of caution: The Stramaglia trail can become very wet and slippery in spring or after heavy rains. Bring boots. Insect repellent as a tick and mosquito preventative is also suggested for the humid months.

Chapter Twelve

Montclair Hawk Watch: Smallest Preserve, Largest Heart

All of one acre in size, the Montclair Hawk Watch is New Jersey Audubon's smallest preserve. It also teaches the largest lesson in a lot of resilience. Previously used for hawk-watching in the 1930s by another local club, the site was purchased in the 1950s by a member of the Montclair Bird Club after the town of Montclair put the parcel up for sale when the owner failed to pay property taxes. The Bird Club reimbursed the member, then donated the site to New Jersey Audubon in 1959. In the 1980s additional property was procured to make access easier for the public.

The Montclair Hawk Watch is the oldest formal bird watch in New Jersey and the second oldest in the country.

Settled in the upper northeast corner of the state, about 15 miles from New York City, the platform perches

**The Montclair
Hawk Watch**
Edgecliff Avenue,
Montclair, NJ

One acre

For information,
contact Scherman-
Hoffman Wildlife
Sanctuary, (908) 766-
5787

Hours: Open to public
September through
November

Best times to visit:
Any time September
through November for
fall hawk migration.

No facilities.

500 feet up a basalt ledge on the First Watchung Mountain Ridge. The sight offers a stunning view of the New York City skyline, from the Verazzano Narrows Bridge connecting New Jersey and Staten Island up to the George Washington Bridge.

TRAILS

There is only one, and that comes as a set of steep steps from the bottom of Edgecliff (now, I wonder why it's called that?) Avenue to the platform. It's a minor challenge, but all you need is a comfortable pair of shoes to make it to the top. You also don't have to worry about poison ivy or any other off-trail perils.

The Montclair Hawk Watch may be New Jersey Audubon's smallest sanctuary but it is one of the largest in terms of the sheer quantity of birds you can see during the fall migration. While songbirds and others are sighted in their travels south, the specialty here is hawk-watching with a capital "H" and "W."

Because of its height and geographic position, the ledge is one of the most perfect spots in the state to enjoy the fall hawk migration. More than 17,000 birds were once recorded passing through the area—in one day!

The migration usually starts in September and runs through November. What you see depends on when you go. From early September to early October, expect to see broad-winged hawks, sharp-shinned and Cooper's hawks, ospreys, early merlins, and

How to Get Here

From all Directions: Find your way to the Garden State Parkway and follow that to Exit 151 (Watchung Avenue). Follow Watchung Avenue west about two miles to its end at Upper Mountain Avenue in Montclair. Turn left onto Bradford Avenue. Turn right onto Edgecliff Road and park on the shoulder.

American Kestrels. Peregrine falcons join the migration in October, and in November there is an increase in the numbers of red-shouldered and red-tailed hawks. At any time you might also be treated to a bald eagle soaring on the air currents.

Another treat? Delicate Monarch butterflies, as they, too, fly south toward Mexico for the winter.

On the Lookout

Chapter Thirteen

Twin Islands Preserve:
Delaware Delight

Sitting in the middle of the Delaware River not far from the Delaware Memorial Bridge and the busy industrial Cherry Hill/Philadelphia area, this 231-acre area comprises two islands: Chester Island, which is to the left if you're facing the river, and Monds Island, near the riverbank dike. Monds has a bald eagle nest and a heron rookery, both of which are visible in the early spring.

There is no access to the islands, unless you want to paddle out. You can view both islands from a small park, but be warned: The park is secluded, and while it is a popular fishing spot, unsavory characters have been known to frequent the area. Use caution if you come here.

This side trip can be done after birding in Rancocas or the Rancocas side trips mentioned in Chapter Six.

**Twin Islands
Preserve**
Greenwich and
Logan Townships

231 acres

For more informa-
tion call Scherman-
Hoffman Wildlife
Sanctuary, (908)
766-5787

Hours: Open daily
from dawn to dusk

Spring Wildflowers

How to Get Here

Take Route 295 to the Repaupo exit (Route 684) and
follow west to where it turns into Floodgate Road.
Continue west to a T-intersection (along the Delaware
River), and turn right into the park. Bear left up the
dirt road and follow it to the floodgates.

Chapter Fourteen

The Hirair and Anna
Hovnanian Preserve:
Pine Barrens Beauty

The 465-acre Hirair and Anna Hovnanian Sanctuary was donated to the Society in 1987 by developer Hirair Hovnanian.

Set at the northern section of New Jersey's pine barrens, Hovnanian offers the best of this scruffy, scrubby terrain, which is unlike any other part of New Jersey.

This trip can be done alone, or as a side trip to either the Sandy Hook Bird Observatory or Cape May.

TRAILS

Hovnanian offers four access trails. They are all a soft walk, meandering through forests resplendent with several types of pine, including pitch and Virginia. Wildflowers, especially in the spring, include sweet pepperbush, pyxie moss, turkeybeard, and the pert sheep laurel.

The Hirair and Anna Hovnanian Preserve
Berkeley Township

465 acres

For information, contact the Rancocas Nature Center, (609) 261-2495

Hours: Dawn to dusk year-round

Best times to visit:
May and early June for warblers; October and November for fall birding.

No facilities.

May and early June are the best months if you're out for birds, especially warblers. Prairie warblers, pine warblers, ovenbirds, and common yellowthroats can be heard or seen throughout May. The rest of the 80-plus species include cedar waxwings, brown thrashers, chipping sparrows, yellow-billed cuckoos, and both red- and white-breasted nuthatches.

The preserve is also harbor to numerous reptiles and amphibians, including the eastern hog-nosed snake, pine snake, and corn snake.

Unlike other preserves, like Old Farm Sanctuary, Hovnanian has no marked trails. Because the trails merge and converge in all directions, it's wise not to go alone; if you do, mark the trail. Luckily, the sand is soft enough to mark off arrows with your foot if it comes to that. Or, if conditions permit, you'll be able to find your own tracks and follow them.

A word of caution: The Pine Barrens is Tick Heaven. I was so enthralled with my surroundings that I neglected to do a fast tick check before jumping into my car, only to find two—Papa and Baby Deer Tick—had hitchhiked a ride on my jeans.

How to Get Here

From North and South: Hovnanian is only two miles
from the Garden State Parkway off Exit 80. Follow the
exit to Route 530 West, bearing left at the light. Proceed
through the next light. A sign for the preserve is on the
right. There is no formal parking lot; park by the sign
and walk down the road to the first access road.

Pine, Hovnanian Preserve

Chapter Fifteen

Bennett Bogs:
The Oldest Sanctuary

Bennett Bogs is one of those places you go to when you really want to enjoy a peaceful, easy stroll while experiencing local beauty. Comanaged by New Jersey Audubon and the Nature Conservancy, the bogs offer visitors a keen look at more than 250 plant species found in the area, including the Pine Barrens Gentian.

The bogs also give you a sense of history. According to New Jersey Audubon, the bogs first came to the attention of the Philadelphia Botanical Club in the early 1900s when botanists identified more than a dozen species of plants that had reached their northern range. Three acres of the bogs were the first grounds deeded to New Jersey Audubon in 1950 and another three were purchased five years later. The Nature Conservancy purchased 18 adjoining acres between 1984 and 1986, to make the bogs what they are today.

Bennett Bogs
Lower Township
Cape May County, NJ

24 acres

For more information, contact Northwood Center at (908)766-5787

Hours: Dawn to dusk year-round

Taking a Closer Look

How to Get Here

To get here, follow Route 647 west to Shunpike Road. The parking lot is on Shunpike.

Appendix A:
Recommended Reading

Boyd, Howard. 1991. *A Field Guide to the Pine Barrens of New Jersey: Its Flora, Fauna, Ecology and Historic Sites*. Medford, New Jersey: Plexus Publishing.

Boyd, Howard. 1997. *A Pine Barrens Odyssey: A Naturalist's Year in the Pine Barrens*. Medford, New Jersey: Plexus Publishing.

Boyd, Howard. 2001. *Wildflowers of the Pine Barrens of New Jersey*. Medford, New Jersey: Plexus Publishing.

Boyle, William J., Jr. 2002. *A Guide to Bird Finding in New Jersey*. New Brunswick, New Jersey: Rutgers University Press.

Collins, Beryl Robichaud, and Karl Anderson. 1994. *Plant Communities of New Jersey: A Study in Landscape Diversity.* New Brunswick, New Jersey: Rutgers University Press.

Davis, Millard C. 1997. *Natural Pathways of New Jersey: A Look at 100 of New Jersey's Finest Natural Places.* Medford, New Jersey: Plexus Publishing, Inc.

Sibley, David. 1987. *The Birds of Cape May.* Bernardsville, New Jersey: Audubon Society.

Walsh, Joan, Vince Elia, Richard Kane, and Thomas Haliwell. 1999. *Birds of New Jersey.* Bernardsville, New Jersey: New Jersey Audubon Society.

Appendix B:
Recommended Web Sites

http://www.bigpockets.com. This Web site is an excellent place to purchase all the clothing and gear needed for outdoors activity in any weather.

http://www.highlandscoalition.org. The official Web site of the Highlands Coalition, a grassroots movement seeking to protect the New Jersey Highlands. A good source for background as well as visitor information.

http://www.njaudubon.org. The official Web site of the New Jersey Audubon Society. Information is provided on all of the nature centers, rare bird alerts, and conservation/environmental efforts throughout the state.

http://www.state.nj.us/pinelands. Information on the New Jersey Pinelands as provided by the state of New Jersey.

About the Author

Born in Paterson, New Jersey, Patricia Robinson is a life-long resident of the Garden State. She has been a freelance travel writer, a public relations executive, a trade magazine editor, and, most recently, a reporter/photographer for a chain of award-winning weekly newspapers in Central Jersey. Her writing and photos have appeared in numerous publications, including the *Christian Science Monitor* and *Nature Photographer*, and she has exhibited her photography at various New Jersey Audubon nature centers throughout the state. Her historical novel, *Declan's Night*, was published by White Mountain Publications in 1992. She is a New Jersey Audubon member.

Index

More Great Books from Plexus Publishing

NATURAL PATHWAYS OF NEW JERSEY

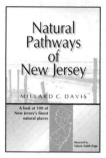

By Millard C. Davis

"Laden with keen observations of the unspoiled world, and the feelings these evoke in Davis, Natural Pathways of New Jersey *represents a rare and genial wedding of science and heart."*

—*The Central Record*

Natural Pathways of New Jersey describes in eloquent detail over 100 natural places in New Jersey. Davis's descriptions of beaches, forests, and fields include not only the essence of the landscapes, but also portray the animals and vegetation native to the area.

Natural Pathways of New Jersey is divided into sections by county, making it very readable and easy for anyone to find the cited areas. The book includes over 100 original watercolor illustrations by artist Valerie Smith-Pope and two simple trips that anyone can take, showcasing the best that New Jersey has to offer.

271 pp/softbound/ISBN 0-937548-35-9/$19.95

A PINE BARRENS ODYSSEY: A NATURALIST'S YEAR IN THE PINE BARRENS OF NEW JERSEY

By Howard P. Boyd

A Pine Barrens Odyssey is a detailed perspective of the seasons in the Pine Barrens of New Jersey. Primarily focused on the chronology of the natural features of the Pine Barrens, this book is meant as a companion to Howard P. Boyd's *A Field Guide to the Pine Barrens of New Jersey* (also available from Plexus).

The two books form an appealing collection for anyone interested in the Pine Barrens of New Jersey. The *Field Guide* can be used as a reference tool for the types of flora and fauna and the *Odyssey* as a calendar of what to expect and look for season by season in this beautiful natural area of New Jersey.

275 pp/softbound/ISBN 0-937548-34-0/$19.95

WILDFLOWERS OF THE PINE BARRENS OF NEW JERSEY

By Howard P. Boyd

Howard P. Boyd offers readers 150 detailed descriptions and 130 color photographs of the most commonly seen Pine Barrens wildflower species. Other useful features include a chapter on the flora of New Jersey, notes on threatened and endangered species, a primer on flower anatomy, a glossary of terms, references to literature cited and recommended reading, and indexes to both the common and scientific names of wildflower species. The author has avoided highly technical language and employed a useful chronological organization (by blossoming times).

176 pp/softbound/ISBN 0-937548-45-6/$19.95

GATEWAY TO AMERICA
World Trade Center Memorial Edition

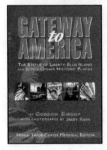

By Gordon Bishop • Photographs by Jerzy Koss

Gateway to America is both a comprehensive guidebook and history. It covers the historic New York/New Jersey triangle that was the window for America's immigration wave in the 19th and 20th centuries. In addition to commemorating the World Trade Center, the book explores Ellis Island, The Statue of Liberty, and six other Gateway landmarks including Liberty State Park, Governors Island, Battery City Park, South Street Seaport, Newport, and the Gateway National Recreational Area. A must for history buffs and visitors to the area alike.

188 pp/softbound/ISBN 0-937548-44-8/$19.95

To order or for a catalog: 609-654-6500, Fax Order Service: 609-654-4309

Plexus Publishing, Inc.

143 Old Marlton Pike • Medford • NJ 08055
E-mail: info@plexuspublishing.com
www.plexuspublishing.com

**NEW JERSEY
AUDUBON
SOCIETY**

Discount on NJAS membership with the purchase of this book! (Next page for details)

The New Jersey Audubon Society (NJAS) is a privately supported, statewide non-profit membership organization dedicated to the preservation of New Jersey's wildlife and natural lands. Founded in 1897, NJAS is one of the oldest and most highly respected Audubon societies in the nation, working in unison with, but completely independent of, the National Audubon Society.

Through a three-fold mission of conservation, research, and education, NJAS fosters environmental awareness and a conservation ethic; protects New Jersey's birds, animals, and plants, especially endangered and threatened species, and promotes the preservation of New Jersey's natural habitats.

NJAS has helped saved many of New Jersey's most treasured places, including the Pinelands, Island Beach State Park, Bear Swamp, and thousands of acres of the New Jersey Highlands and Delaware Bay Shore. We were a driving force behind the Freshwater Wetlands Protection Act, one of the strongest wetlands laws in the nation, and the Garden State Preservation Trust Act, which will protect one million acres during this decade. And we helped shape nearly every other act of conservation legislation in the state.

Support the preservation of New Jersey's wildlife and natural lands. Become a member of the New Jersey Audubon Society by returning the membership form on the back of this page, visiting our website at <u>www.njaudubon.org</u>, or calling (908) 204-8998.

INFORMATION FILED WITH THE ATTORNEY GENERAL CONCERNING THIS CHARITABLE SOLICITATION MAY BE OBTAINED FROM THE ATTORNEY GENERAL OF THE STATE OF NEW JERSEY BY CALLING (973-504-6215). REGISTRATION WITH THE ATTORNEY GENERAL DOES NOT IMPLY ENDORSEMENT.

Membership in the New Jersey Audubon Society provides great benefits:

Aside from the satisfaction you get from helping to preserve New Jersey's wildlife and wild places, all members receive:

√ Membership card and window decal,
√ Discounts on NJAS store merchandise and field trips,
√ Quarterly issues of *New Jersey Audubon* magazine.
√ *New Jersey Birds* and *Green Gram Online Action Alert* are also available upon request.
√ Become a member at the $250 level or higher and receive invitations to special field trips and events.
√ Life Members receive all of the above plus a listing in our magazine and annual report.

- -

☐ **YES!** I want to become a member of the New Jersey Audubon Society and help save New Jersey's wildlife and natural lands.

New Member Name/s
_____

Address
_____

City	State	Zip Code

☐ Individual ....$35   ☐ Goldfinch $250
☐ Family ....$45   ☐ Golden Eagle $500
☐ Friend ....$100   ☐ Life Member:.............$2,000

Special discount with book purchase:

☐ Individual ....$25   ☐ Family $35

Please send me: ☐ *New Jersey Birds*
☐ *Green Gram On-line Action Alert* (E-mail address_____)

☐ Check	☐ MasterCard	☐ Visa

Cardholder Name
_____

Card Number   Expiration Date

Please fill out and return this form with your tax-deductible membership contribution to the **New Jersey Audubon Society, PO Box 126, 9 Hardscrabble Road, Bernardsville, New Jersey 07924** • Tel (908) 204-8998 • www.njaudubon.org.